JUST WRITE!

Practical Advice for Writing Your Story

By

James Mascia

Published by James Mascia at Dren Productions LLC
1st edition ©2016
Copyright 2016 by James Mascia at Dren Productions
Published in the United States of America

This is for all the people who have ever put a pen to paper to tell an incredible story.

"When I sit down to write a book, I do not say to myself, 'I am going to produce a work of art.' I write it because there is some lie that I want to expose, some fact to which I want to draw attention, and my initial concern is to get a hearing."

- George Orwell

"We do not need magic to change the world, we carry all the power we need inside ourselves already."

- J.K. Rowling

Table of Contents

Putting Off Until Tomorrow

Recently, an old college friend told me how proud he was of me. He explained how he always hears people talking about how they want to write a book, paint, sculpt, become a poet, but they never get it done. He was amazed that I said I was going to write, and that I actually did it, and not only that, but I continue doing it.

That got me thinking that the only real difference between a writer and someone who aspires to be a writer is that a writer doesn't put off until tomorrow what they can do today.

The biggest excuse one always hears about someone wanting to write a book, is that they don't have the time to do it. The truth is, I think, these people don't want to make the time to do it.

Let me tell you, I am a teacher, so, I work my 40+ hours a week, but I also tutor on the side for probably another 15 – 20 hours a week. Two or three weekends a month, I get in the car and travel to some destination for a comic book convention where I sell my books and comics. Oh, and to add to that, I have an insane three-year-old (for those of you who are parents, you know what I'm talking about). So, if anyone has an excuse that they do not have any time to write, it is me.

Now, I'm not saying all this to brag. I'm trying to give you an idea. If I can get in at least a little bit of writing every day, than anyone can. The point is, that you have to do it instead of saying, "I'll get to it when I have the time."

It isn't that hard to get started. If someone wants to write a book, they must have an idea in mind. The fact is, they have to sit at that keyboard—or, like in my case, a pen and notebook—and get those ideas out of their head. (Yes, for those of you wondering, before I type my stories out on the computer, I write them in a book. That way when I copy it down onto the computer, it forces me to edit as I go.)

Many people probably think that they have to get all their ideas out at once. That is definitely not the case. I set a daily writing goal for myself. My goal is not that big—only 500 words a day. That isn't a lot. If you're typing in standard font, and single spaced pages, this is only one page. So, my goal is really one page a day. That's 3,500 words a week. Most days, I exceed that goal. However, there are days where I won't make it. But that's okay, because I will still make my goal by the end of the week.

If writing is your passion, you should make time to do it. Life happens. But if this is something you truly want to do, it is important that you get it done. Inventory your time management. Maybe there is some time in the evening when you could write something while you're sitting in front of the TV. I like to write early in the morning before work, or late at night right before bed. Maybe you can start just by writing for one hour each day on the weekends and expand from there.

The important thing is to get it done. Stop saying that you don't have the time. Make the time. Then maybe you will have a friend tell you how proud they are of you.

Find Your Passion

Writing doesn't have to be a chore—and to be frank, if you do see it as a chore, you probably shouldn't be writing.

Think about this. Have you ever read a book by one of your favorite authors and just couldn't get into it? Did you feel that something was off about the writing when compared to his/her other books? Why do you think that is?

While you could accuse the author of being a hack, the truth is they've lost their passion for what they were writing.

When an author writes something they are truly passionate about, when they enjoy writing their story, that passion and enjoyment is conveyed to the reader. Even the best authors can get bogged down with life that they begin to see their writing as a chore. It's those moments when their writing becomes mediocre at best.

You have to feel what you're writing. There has to be passion behind it. If that goes away, you need to do something else. Because if you are bored with what you're writing, and if you are finding it difficult to get through, I assure you that any potential reader is going to feel the same way when they pick up your book (and immediately put it back down).

I know this sounds contrary to the "just do it" mentality I discussed in the previous section. I assure you this is not the case. I'm saying that if what you're writing right now isn't grabbing you, go write something else.

It took me two years to finish the first draft to the fifth and final book of my *High School Heroes* series. Part of this was the fact that I was getting used to having a baby around the house, and was trying to figure out a new routine for writing that wouldn't interfere with my time with him. The rest of it was that after writing the series for so long (six years since I had begun the first book), I was almost losing interest in my own story. So, I dropped it, and took a break—twice.

That's not to say I stopped writing altogether. I didn't. Instead, I began some other projects. Once I had a long enough break from *High School Heroes* (really, only a few weeks each time). I jumped right back into the story with a renewed passion.

Understand that if your writing feels tedious, if you are starting to see doing another 500 words of a story as a chore, it's okay to step back for a while and come back to it later. What is important though is that you not drop it altogether. I cannot stress this enough.

There are so many people out there that have half-finished stories, and it's because they lost interest, or thought it was too hard, or think they've written themselves into a corner. While it's okay to step back for a while and write something different, you must go back to it eventually. Don't abandon the story in the middle, only to die a tragic death in your own imagination. Don't give up on it, even if you feel there is nowhere else to go. Any story can be fixed, or saved, if you have the passion to do so.

If you truly feel there is nowhere left to go in a story, read back through it, and think of some changes you can make to it to take it in a new direction. This can bring a refreshed hope to the story.

Now, I do have to say that if you find yourself with several different abandoned projects, that you need to buckle down and pick one to finish. And I'm not talking about writing it just for the sake of writing. That would lead to telling a mediocre story like I mentioned earlier. Instead, grab hold of one of those abandoned projects and re-ignite that passion somehow.

Try one of these options to get that passion back.

GET A WRITING COACH

I only put this first because it is the easiest. It is something that I have tried once, and it worked out very well, but it isn't something I ever went back to. This is the one item on this list that will likely cost you money.

A writing coach doesn't have to cost you a lot of money (it can cost you a lot, but it doesn't have to). Do a Google search for "Writing Coaches." There is also a website called Fiverr.com, which will allow you to get something like a writing coach (among other things, but that's for later) starting at only $5.

What I like about writing coaches is that you are paying them to help you, and they are going to do their best to do that. The individualized attention is a plus and can range from just some general advice and feedback on your writing, all the way up to giving you an entire schedule and forcing you to adhere to it.

The important thing when seeking a writing coach is that you find someone who you not only get along with, but who will also understand your writing. You don't want to get mixed up with someone who is going to make you change your entire story just because they don't agree with it. That's the fastest way to get discouraged and lose your passion.

POST YOUR STORY ONLINE

Sometimes, all we need just a little feedback on our writing to get us back on track. This is where online forums come in. There are some good websites that will get you some valuable feedback.

The ones that I like and find helpful include:

> Authonomy.com – This one is owned by HarperCollins. Not only can you put your work online and get that feedback, but each month HarperCollins selects five manuscripts for possible publication. So, this one is a win all around. https://www.authonomy.com

> AbsoluteWrite.com – I like this site because not only can you show off your writing, but it also suggests writing prompts, writing discussions (narrowed down by genre), and other wonderful tips. It is definitely worth a look at. https://www.absolutewrite.com

MyWritersCircle.com – This one is similar to Absolute Write; there is more to it than simply writing feedback, but the feedback here is usually quite valuable. They also offer writing challenges that you can participate in that might help inspire your muse. https://www.mywriterscircle.com

Fanstory.com – I include this on the list because it is a good site for feedback in any genre (even though there is a huge focus on fan-fiction). They also run cool contests on this site . The thing I don't like about this site is that you have to pay, and I'm of the mindset that if you can get the same thing for free somewhere else, why should I have to pay for it? https://www.fanstory.com

Two things that you have to remember about posting to these online sites:

You can get some knuckleheads leaving rude comments on your story, which can get discouraging and isn't going to help you at all. As Alfred once said to Batman, "Some men just like to watch the world burn." I equate these trolls to those people. They make negative comments simply to make you feel bad and starting a virtual fight. It is best to ignore those people instead of engaging with them.

More important is that to get valuable feedback, you have to GIVE valuable feedback. When others see that you are not on these sites just for yourself, they are more willing to help you out. So, before you even post something of your own, I would jump onto these sites and read through some other and give them your opinion.

FIND A LOCAL WRITING GROUP

Personally, I like this better than the online forums. With a live group rather than online, you get face to face contact when getting feedback, and you can ask questions that can be answered then and there, leading to true discussions about your work.

I find that this interaction can be more motivating than reading comments online. I also find that people are more likely to give constructive feedback in an "up-close and personal" setting than they are on the computer.

Being in a writing group also will allow you to practice reading your work aloud, which is something all writers should know how to do, and if this is something you need to work on (I definitely did when I was starting out). This is the perfect place to do it, and you can get feedback from your audience.

The downside is that most writing groups meet (at most) two times a month. My own writing group meets once per month. This means you might have to wait a few weeks to get the feedback on that piece.

Check for these groups at your library or local college, many of them meet (or at least recruit) new members. You can also try doing a search online, but I can't promise that will work in every area.

READ SOMETHING SIMILAR

Yes, that's right. Sometimes getting that passion back requires you to read a little. Seeing what other authors are doing in your genre can be a great motivator to getting you back on track.

The important thing to remember is, that though you want to read, you also want to make sure that you are writing as well. It's very easy to get caught up in the reading and forget that you do have something to do.

If none of these work, find what works best for you. There must be something out there that can ignite that passion and get you back to writing.

Characters:

When you begin a story, you should know about your characters. When I create my characters, I will try to do an outline about them. This section is specifically designed for you to get to know your characters. There are a couple of techniques that you can use, and you can use one, or all of them. The important thing is, that you do some writing about your character before you really get into the meat of your story.

These techniques will help you develop a background and personality for your character. By doing some of these techniques when I was writing my *High School Heroes* series, I actually came up with plot points for the novels as well as ideas for some side stories about my characters. So, you never know how this might help you.

Another way to get to know your character is by using the Journal Writing Prompts section of this book and writing as if you are your character. It is a great way to get into your character's head.

Now, you may notice that we are focusing on characters before we focus on plot. I happen to do it thi way. If you feel like you need to have a solid plot before you do this section, then by all means, go to that section first and then return here.

CHARACTER SHEET:

As you begin looking through this section, there are a few important rules for using this character sheet.

I encourage you to copy and print the character sheet. That's what it's here for. If I didn't want you to use it, I wouldn't have put it in the book. So, copy, copy, copy.

Speaking of copies, make a copy for each of the main character in your story. You might even want to do this for some of your minor characters as well (I personally have learned things about some of my minor characters by filling this out for them).

As you fill out the sheet, keep in mind that everything is optional. If you don't think you can fill in one of the sections, simply skip it. This is just an exercise to let you get to know your characters, not cause you more stress.

Have fun with it.

Title of Book/Story:				
Character Name:		Name Origin/Meaning:		
Nickname(s):		Does character like nickname(s):		

Hair Color:	Eye Color:	Height:	Weight:	Age:

Birthday:	Place of Birth:	Ethnicity:	Religion:

Brief Description of Home:

Brief Description of Family:

What did/does character want to be when he/she grew up?	Current Occupation:	Job Satisfaction Level:

Marital/Relationship Status:	Sexual Orientation:

Who do people say this character looks like?	Any distinguishing marks (freckles, moles, tattoos, scars, etc.):

Briefly describe what this character thinks of him/herself (looks, personality, place in world, etc.):

Explain how the character dresses (expensive, conservative, sexy, trashy, sporty, cheap, etc.):	Explain why they dress this way:	
Gestures:	Posture:	Habits:

Briefly describe a typical day in the life of your character:		
Earliest Memory:	Happiest Memory:	Saddest Memory:

Most significant childhood event:	Any past/current major illnesses:	
First romance/crush:	First sexual experience (was it positive or negative):	
Character's Best Friend:	Other Friends:	Describe how character relates to friends:

How character relates to strangers:	How character relates to same sex:	How character relates to opposite sex:
How character relates to children:	How character relates to authority:	How character relates to competitors:

Character is most comfortable when:	Character is most uncomfortable when:
Character's most embarrassing moment:	Character's deepest desire:
The one thing character values most:	Character's personal philosophy:
Character's greatest strength:	Other positive attributes:
Character's greatest flaw:	Other negative attributes:
Proudest accomplishment:	Biggest regret:

QUESTIONS FOR YOUR

CHARACTER:

Conducting an interview with your character is another great way you can get to know them. This section provides 50 suggested questions. You may notice that some of the questions will overlap with what is on the chart, that's okay. As with the chart, this section has a couple of rules.

Just like the chart, feel free to copy this.

Don't try to answer all the questions. Pick 10–15 for your character to answer. There is a fine line between fleshing out your character and stalling the actual writing of your book.

Think of it like an interview. As you respond, think about your character's voice. Write the response as if your character were speaking right in front of you.

Don't worry about being grammatically correct. Remember, this is an exercise, not actually writing a novel.

Try to give more than a couple words for an answer (unless that is a part of your character's voice).

Feel free to come up with your own questions. There is no reason you should stop with the 50 I provided. You can ask your character virtually anything. This is to give you some ideas.

Once again, have fun with it.

1) Where were you born? Tell me what you can remember about it.
2) Describe yourself in 10 words or less.
3) Describe your parents or whoever raised you. Should they have been more lenient or strict with you?
4) Name five things your parents say/said to you all the time.
5) How do you celebrate your birthday?
6) How do you celebrate holidays? What holiday is most celebrated in your home?
7) List ten places you'd like to visit before you die. Why pick those places?
8) Who would you consider to be one of your heroes?
9) Who do you have absolutely no respect for?
10) How have you changed in the last ten years?
11) Do you make friends easily? Why or why not?
12) When you were a child, what did you want to be when you grew up? Did that change? If so, what do you want to be now?
13) What is your favorite TV show? Movie? Book? Video game? Music? Sport?
14) Describe the teacher you believe had the greatest impact on your life.
15) Describe the most difficult decision you have had to make in your life.
16) What was the most important day in your life? Why did it have such a significant impact on you?
17) Are you at all concerned with how other people feel about you? Why or why not?
18) What is your favorite pig-out food?
19) What is the meaning of life?
20) Where is your favorite place for some quiet, alone time? Describe it.
21) How many boyfriends/girlfriends have you had? Do you think that's a lot? Is dating important to you?
22) When did you realize, or how will you know when you have fallen in love?
23) Describe something that will make you laugh every time.
24) Describe something that will make you cry every time.
25) How old were you when you lost your virginity? Was it good?
26) What is the stupidest thing you have ever done?
27) Do you know how to cook? If so, how did you learn? If not, how do you feed yourself?
28) When you come home at the end of the day, how do you feel? Why?
29) Name your three closest friends and describe each of them. Who do you consider your best friend and why?
30) Describe the pets you had growing up. Do you have similar pets today? Why or why not?
31) What is the thing that annoys you the most? What do you do when you are annoyed?
32) Describe the television commercial that makes you the angriest. Why does it make you feel that way?
33) When the aliens land on Earth, who will be the first person they talk to?
34) If you could be any animal, which animal would you be? Why?
35) If you could go back in time to relive any point in your life, where would you go? Why?
36) If you could go back in time to change any point in your life, where would you go? Why?
37) When you are looking for inspiration, where do you look? Why?
38) What are your greatest fears?
39) What will you do when the zombie apocalypse comes?

40) If you could ask God any question, what would it be?

41) What subject in school do you think was your best? Your worst? Why?

42) Describe a practical joke you played on someone. Was it worth it? Why or why not?

43) If you have to do research, are you more likely to go to the library, Google or Wikipedia? Why?

44) Describe the side of you that no one else ever sees.

45) What do you believe is the magic formula for success?

46) If you were a man/woman, how would your life have been different?

47) What would you consider to be your greatest strength? Your greatest flaw?

48) What do you enjoy more: going out on the town, or spending an evening at home? Why?

49) If you ruled the world, how would things be different?

50) What do you think it means to "have it all?"

How to Reveal a Character's Emotions

He felt angry. She felt sad. They were excited.

Yes, you are telling the emotions of the characters in the story, but this really doesn't show us anything important, and frankly, unless you are writing for a preschool audience, its boring.

Take your favorite novel, and read a scene in it that is emotionally charged (it can be a heated argument, or a romantic love scene. It doesn't matter.) Look at how the author shows the sentiments of characters within that scene. They don't simply say how the character is feeling, or if they do, they go beyond that to show the reader exactly how angry, sad, happy, etc. they are. In writing, you need to do that as well. This is one of those cases where you have to *show* the characters emotions instead of *telling* about them.

In order to really *show* the emotions in a way that doesn't simply state, "He felt angry," you can do a number of things.

Delve Deep into Your Character's Mind

Like real human beings, your characters have inner thoughts that they share with no one. However, as a writer, you can let your readers in on those inner thoughts. This will require you to get into your character's head.

Try and feel the emotion from your character's point of view. For example, I'll continue on the emotion of anger. As you write your scene:

Think about what is making your character angry and why.

Think about what your character realizes about his or her own anger.

Think about what the character wants to happen to resolve this anger.

Think about what your character would like to do to the person/or thing that is making him or her angry.

Think about what other conflicting emotions this character might have.

Then construct a paragraph or two in which you describe all these things. And as an extra challenge, try to do it without ever once saying what the emotion is. Look at the following, short example.

Why did she have to be so cruel? It wasn't the boy's fault that he couldn't do it, yet she expected him to be the next Rembrandt or Picasso. It wasn't the fact that she expected so much of the boy that had him out of sorts, it was more that she was punishing him for getting it wrong. He wished she would just leave him alone. He wanted to scream at her, but he couldn't do it in front of the boy, what would he think if he saw his father coming and shouting in his mother's face? He pushed it back down into the pit of his stomach, where he knew it would fester until eventually he'd explode.

You get the feeling that he is angry, but we do it completely in his mind with his inner thoughts. We also have a much deeper story that gets into what the character is actually feeling, rather than only saying, "He was angry."

Make the Character Do Something
Another way you can show your character's emotions is by having them perform some action when they are feeling the emotion. This can be something that they do in only this specific situation, or it can be a quirk that they do every time they feel this way.

Feel what your character is feeling. Think about your own reactions to this. Do your palms get sweaty when you're nervous? Do your cheeks get hot when you're embarrassed or angry? Do you shake uncontrollably with laughter when you're excited? Then, as you write your scene:

Think about if you'd want your character to react the same way as you.

Think about what physical action they could do when they feel this emotion.

Think about what would set him or her apart from other characters in the same situation.

Think about how your character might overreact to the situation.

Then construct a paragraph or two in which you describe all these things. Again, as an extra challenge, try to do it without ever once saying what the emotion is. Look at the following, short example.

His cheeks heated up and he knew they had already turned bright red. His fists clenched tightly, but he made sure to keep his arms firmly at his sides so he wouldn't throw something, or punch a hole through a wall like he did last time. Still, his arms shook with the need to act. They burned with the desire to cause some destruction. Only when he let loose would the feeling go away.

Again, we understand perfectly that this character is angry, but we have gone well beyond actually stating this fact. We get a description that gives us a deeper meaning behind this anger.

Use Dialogue

The last way is using dialogue. Now, I will say that dialogue shouldn't be used by itself (unless you are writing a play, and even then, you'd have some stage directions for the actors). But you can convey the emotion through dialogue without the character actually saying, "This is how I feel."

Again, you need to put yourself into a similar situation, and you almost have to "perform" both sides of the conversation (or only one side if the character talks to himself/herself.) What would you say? What would they say? Would their personality make them open to this conversation, or would they try to avoid it? As you write your scene:

Think about what needs to be said in the conversation.

Think about how the character's words (or inflections) might change with different emotions.

Think about the character's reaction to the previous line of dialogue.

Think about what your character really wants.

Then construct a conversation where all these things are considered. Again, as an extra challenge, try to do it without ever once saying what the emotion is. Look at the following, short example. For the purpose of this example, I will be focusing on the dialogue, in my story I would intersperse this with what I had already stated in the previous sections.

"You smell like you've taken a bath in it, Paul. How many did you have? How many?"
"Not enough apparently."
"When? When are you going to wake up and realize we're not kids anymore? You have—"
"Don't give me this crap again, Jane."
"I have to. You never learn. You never listen. One night I'm going to get a call because you've gotten yourself killed. Then where will I be. Where will we be?"
"You don't understand."
"Then tell me. Tell me why you'd rather go out to a bar every night than stay here with me? Are you even attracted to me anymore?"
"Of course."
"No. You're only attracted to the bottle you're drinking from. And I'm done with it, Paul. I'm done with you."

As I said, I concentrated on only the dialogue, and hopefully that was enough to paint a picture in your head. The words should be enough to tell you the emotions of the characters. But if you were to have Paul throw his hands up in the air when he says, "Not enough apparently," or have Jane pause and reflect a moment after he says, "You don't understand," and you have yourself quite an emotional scene.

Also, notice the two distinct voices. Notice that Jane speaks a lot, and that she repeats her words twice, many times. This can be written in as a character quirk for her, and adds depth not only to the scene, but her character. Paul is only speaking in short phrases. you could also add a reason for that. Maybe you can have Jane notice that he's hardly speaking, and that he only does that when he's embarrassed by what he's done. It's completely up to you, but the possibilities are endless.

There are any number of ways that you can show emotions in your characters. These three things are but a sampling of what you can do. The important thing to remember, is that you need to go way beyond just saying how the character is feeling.

Creating Fictional Worlds

When people create the world of their story, they are thinking about the setting. While that is the most major part of the world, it isn't the only factor. It has to do with the people, their attitudes, their mannerisms, etc. It also has to do with the stuff within the setting, the technology, the government, and many other things.

Whether you are writing a romance or creating a *Lord of the Rings* type fantasy, you need to create a world for your story.

Yes, you can set your story in a real place. However, if you set your story in New York City it's very different than if you set it in Wichita or even San Diego. If it's someplace you live, great! You already have a leg up on what we're going to talk about in this section. If however, it is someplace you don't live, or if it's an entirely new place you are creating, you need to set rules for this world.

I call them "rules," but what I mean is just a normal routine, because every place in this world and beyond there are different expectations for behavior. Some of these rules are written, such as laws and other legalities, and some are not. For instance, in New York City, if you stand on a curb and hold your hand up you are probably hailing a taxi cab. It is an unwritten rule of that world. Standing on a curb and holding up your hand in East Dixon, Nowhere, is not going to mean the same thing.

Breaking it down further, there are different rules for professions. A person working at Starbucks is going to have different set of rules than someone who works in the subway. Just like there is going to be a different set of rules if your characters' world is an office building on Wall Street compared to if their world revolves around Capitol Hill in Washington DC.

And then we have to consider the "when" of the story. Things are different today than they were in the 1950s, just as it will be different in the 2050s. If you aren't setting your story in modern day (or even if you are) you have to consider the things that make that era unique.

If you are writing something set in the past, do some research (start with Google), look at the lifestyles of those people. Look at the types of jobs that were held in high regard. Look for specific things like who was President, or mayor at the time (if set in a real place). Look at the types of cars they drove. All of these things, among others will help build your world.

This is also true for fantasy worlds. Where the story takes place and the rules of this purely fictional world will affect the story and the characters in it. Think about the rules of that world and what makes it different from the "real" world. If you are setting this in a fantasy world, there better be some major differences than the world we live in today.

Again whether it's romance, historical drama, science fiction, thriller, etc., here are some questions to ask yourself. Keep in mind that while all of these questions might not directly apply to your story, answering them may still add depth and may generate more ideas for a new direction to take it in. You will notice that none of the questions will have anything to do with the plot, though they can help lead you toward one.

QUESTIONS

Anywhere

These questions can be used no matter the setting of your story.

What is the setting of your story? Try to be as specific as possible. Describe the place using all five senses.

At first glance, what does this world look like? Is there something underneath the surface that is hidden?

What are the characters' lifestyles like? Are they wealthy, poor, middle-class? Is there a hierarchy among the citizens?

What kind of government rules this world? Is it a democracy or a dictatorship? Or is it something else entirely? How do the people view their leaders?

How are laws enforced in this world? What do they do with criminals?

What is the climate like? Are there multiple climates? Are there seasons?

What kinds of foods to the people eat? Where does the food come from? Consider that foods eaten in France, differ than those in China, differ from those in the United States. You can even break down foods more locally than that.

What resources does this world have in abundance? What is scarce? How do the people obtain these resources?

What is the primary mode of transportation? Is it different, depending on social class?

How do the characters communicate? Are there slang terms they use that is unique to this area?

What is the primary religion in this world? Are their multiple religions? If so how to they interact with each other? Is religion even important in this world?

What flora and fauna are present in this world? Are any of them integrated into the society? If so, how?

Is race important in this world? If so, explain how, and what it means to be a certain race.

What is the most important thing to the society in this world? What isn't valued at all?

What is something that is so commonplace in this world that people living there wouldn't notice it? You can list multiple things here.

Are there any common interests of the people in this world? Hobbies? Jobs?

Fantasy/Sci-Fi Worlds

The following questions are more specific for a world not set in our own reality. However, before you answer these questions, you should still answer the "Anywhere" questions.

At first sight, how is this world different than ours?

Are there people here that aren't human? If so, describe them.

Is there advanced technology in this world? If so, how is it used and for what purpose?

What is the history of the people of this world? What events have shaped their history to bring them to the point in your story? How have these events formed their beliefs and attitudes?

What supernatural elements (if any) exist in this world?

Are humans an intelligent species in this world? If so, are they the ONLY intelligent species?

Does magic exist in this world? If so, how is it viewed? Who can use it? How does the magic work?

MAP IT OUT

When I'm creating a world, whether it is real or not, I always make use of a map. This helps me gauge distances, and lets me see generally how this world is laid out. When I did my novel, *The Island of Dren*, I actually drew a map of what the island looked like, including all major locations and topography (mountains, forests, rivers, etc.) This kept me routed and consistent as the characters travelled from one place to another on the island. Then when I did my novel, *High School Heroes*, I set the story in the real town of Jefferson Hills, Pennsylvania, which is just south of Pittsburgh. I used Google maps when writing this story, so I know things like how far it was from the school to the hospital, or my character's house to Pittsburgh. This gave me realistic travel times, as well as the correct routes to take to get there.

Do you have to be that detailed when creating your world? No. But it does help tell your story, and it does help to keep you consistent.

If you've noticed, I've used the word consistent a couple of times in the previous paragraphs. Consistency is the key. If the characters cross a river on their way someplace, they have to cross that same river on the way back. This is a simple example, and an easy one for you to catch.

It's especially important if you are writing about a real place, which is why I use Google maps. If you are describing a place, and you describe it incorrectly, that is going to be distracting to the people reading your story that are familiar with that place. I remember reading a novel that had several scenes in the Smithsonian museums. I know those museums very well, and the way they were described were so incorrect as far as where things were located and what was inside them, that it actually left a sour taste in my mouth. Luckily, the book itself was still quite good and enjoyable to read, but it was clear that the author had never set foot inside those places. This is what I mean when I use the word consistency.

So, log onto Google Maps (https://maps.google.com) and take a look at the place you are setting your story. For many places, you can actually get all the way down to the street view, so you can pretend like you are driving down that very street. This can really give you an idea of how to describe the setting of the story.

If you are creating a new world, do create a map as well. If you aren't an artist, I suggest going on a website like Fiverr (https://www.fiverr.com) and hiring an artist to draw one for you based on your description. The map will cost as little as $5 for something simple (more if you want something very elaborate). These can be great visual aids when creating your world and while you're writing the story itself.

USE CHARACTERS TO REVEAL YOUR WORLD

So, you're saying to yourself, "Didn't he just do a whole section on character? Then why is he writing about it again?"

These things interlock. You can't create a good plot without both, and sometimes you need one in order to describe the other.

In this case, think about one of your characters (or more than one). Where do they fit in the world of your story? How do they view the world through their eyes? Think about it, not every character will see your world in the same light, and the way your reader perceives this world is largely going to be with how your characters interact with it.

With that in mind, think about how you can reveal your world through your characters. Pick two characters from your story (preferably two characters with vastly different points of view). Then write a paragraph or two in which that character describes the world they live in. How do they feel about your world? Are they an outsider in this world? Did they used to be an outsider? Is there anything they find strange about this world? Is there something they enjoy about this world they would miss if they were gone? Use all these ideas and add more and describe the world. As you describe them, try to use all five senses (or at least as many as you can).

When you've completed that, think about how their view of this world can change. What if they were describing this world while they were incredibly happy (like they just discovered they were in love)? Angry? Depressed? Write more, describing the world again through a range of emotions. These descriptions can actually be used somewhere in your story (with some modifications, of course).

Try this a couple of times as you write your story. The way your character views the world can change from the beginning to the end of the story, and they will be taking the reader along with them on their journey.

A LESSON IN HISTORY

Another thing you must consider, especially when constructing a world that is unlike our own, is the history of that world. You need to do that for real-world stories, but for those, history is already laid out for you, you must only do a little research.

Think about this. Unless your story occurs at the beginning of all time and space, then something had to occur prior to what is happening in your story. Even if you are writing the story of Adam and Eve, there is a history that occurs prior to them coming to the Earth. What is that history?

A backstory is important, not just for your characters, but for the world as well. This backstory is going to influence the events that occur in your book even if they are only briefly mentioned, if at all. Knowing the backstory of your world is almost as important as knowing the basic plot of your story (okay, maybe the backstory is a little less important, but you get where I'm coming from.)

Like in the last section with character, there is a little exercise to go with this section. Pretend you are a historian and chronicle the history of your world for the last 10, 20, 100, or 1,000 years. Essentially, go back as far as you need to go. If you are writing a story set in the 1960s, you might only need to go back 20 years, but if you are writing a grand epic, you may want to consider the last 1,000 years of history. Create a timeline of important events. Highlight ones that you believe will be vital for your story (these are the events that you think will be worth mentioning somewhere in the story). Then figure out how your character personally may have been effected by these particular events, even if they occurred long before they were born. For example, think about how someone born in Hiroshima in the 1990s would have been effected by the atomic bomb being dropped on the city 50 years before they conceived. Just because they weren't there, doesn't mean there is no impact on their lives.

As you create this history for the world, consider that history isn't always perfect. Hell, history itself is barely even logical. The strongest army doesn't always win the war. Countries don't always stay together. Rulers fall out of power. Important people are killed, or simply die, for no reason whatsoever. Don't make your history perfect. Throw some monkey wrenches into it. Think of things that have happened in this world's history that people might not be proud of. Do this and your history will seem more realistic—much more like our own.

Another thing to consider when creating a history is how technology advances. Things changed between the year 0 and the year 1,000 in our world. The same needs to happen for your history. Was there an invention that changed the way the people in your story lived their lives? Was there something invented that proved disastrous, but is still being used? What was the effect of things invented many years prior effect the world today? Include this in your history as well.

So, get out there and create your world's history.

AS YOU WRITE

So, you're writing the story and you want to put all of this glorious detail into your book right up front so that your reader can get into the world of the story with your characters.

The problem with that is… YAWN!

Doing that is boring and is going to make your reader close the book and possibly not ever open it again. We can't all be Tolkien, who was able to include every excruciating detail of his world in his stories. Readers today do not have the patience to stick with you as you lay out pages and pages of description. They want to get to the story and they want to get to it now.

No, I'm not saying that all that hard work you've done in creating this world is now going to go to waste. We just need to find a good way to incorporate it into our story.

As you write, try to do the following three things:

Write only what your characters notice. Don't include the things that are commonplace (unless it's integral to the story). Is your character likely to comment the dogs barking in detail if it's something they hear every day? No, probably not. Think about the things that seem out of place, or out of the ordinary for the character. These are the things you should describe in detail.

Let the description unfold as your character moves through the scene. Instead of having all this description right up front, give it to the reader little by little as the character goes about their business. Think about a child running into a candy store (or toy store if you prefer). What is that child going to notice first? How will they react? How will they interact? Then what will they notice next? Repeat the cycle as the scene unfolds.

Use the setting as an active part of the story. As your character walks into the lobby of a hotel, they can notice a table filled with great, green plants sitting atop it that filled the room with the wonderful smell of a rainforest. But instead of simply telling us the table is there and describing it to our reader, have it be in your character's way and make him/her have to step around it, maybe run his/her fingers through the leaves. Make use of the setting in the scene, instead of simply describing it.

If you can do these things as you do your writing, you will have a full, fleshed-out world, and you will keep your reader engaged. In other words, it is a situation where everyone wins.

Plot:

It doesn't matter how good your characters are if you don't have a halfway decent plot to go along with them. The hardest part, for some people anyway, is trying to find those ideas.

This section of the book is going to deal with generating ideas for your stories, as well as putting them effectively into a worthwhile text. There are any number of ways you can do this, and we are going to discuss a few of them I have found effective.

We are going to start with some ways to generate ideas.

WRITING PROMPTS

One of those ways is by using writing prompts. Toward the end of this book, there are many prompts to get you started. These are great ways just to get that pen to paper, or words on the screen. Sometimes they will generate an idea that will be a part of a larger story, or sometimes they will become the backbone of the story. Either way, I definitely advocate for these prompts.

I myself have used prompts (sometimes my own, and sometimes from others) when I find that I have nothing to write. I have gotten a few short stories out of such prompts, and some ideas for some full length pieces.

See page 29 for the Writing Prompts section of this book.

WRITE WHAT YOU KNOW

People say that experience is the best teacher. That can also be true for your writing as well. You don't have to be writing an autobiography or a memoir to utilize your own experiences in your writing.

For example, I used my day job is as a high school English teacher, to come up with ideas for my *High School Heroes* series. I had a plethora of experiences to add to my book. The way students behave in the cafeteria, to the way some of the teachers think in the book, these all came from my experiences as a teacher. While this isn't the actual basis of my book, it did help flesh out some ideas for the story.

Just because you start off using your own experiences, doesn't mean you can't build a fictional world around it. You might start off with one of your own experiences, but then go into a totally different direction with your characters than you took in real life. Either way, you have a stepping off point for a story.

Think about these five suggestions and see if you are able to build a story around it.

A Death in the Family

Most of us have experienced a death of a close loved one. Think about how you and your relatives all reacted to this event. Was there any animosity toward each other? Did someone get blamed for the person's death? Did someone take the passing worse than others? All of these things can be fuel for a story.

Teenage/College Years

Growing up is hard to do, but it makes for excellent stories. We usually call these "coming of age" stories. So, think back to your teenage years and possibly, early college years. Were there challenges you faced? Were you troubled as a youth? Did you have to deal with bullies? What were your first experiences living on your own? Was there major conflict with your parents? All of these can be used to jumpstart a story (maybe several).

Work Work Work

Our jobs can also bring more to our stories. Everyone has had a boss or supervisor they've absolutely hated, or have been given a completely pointless task to do. Or maybe there was some juicy gossip about a couple of coworkers. You can use these things to develop some details for a story.

Romantic Entanglements

Yup, we're going there. And why are we going there? Because everyone has a story to tell about the dating world. It could be a terrible first date, an extremely funny blind date story, or possibly even a person you dated who wasn't who they claimed they were. It could also be the story of how you fell in love with your soul mate.

Vacation Or Bust

You've seen those road-trip movies. Now, I'm not saying you have experiences like the people in those movies have (well, maybe you do), but vacations can also be great ideas for stories. Have you ever been fooled by online pictures of a hotel only to be totally disgusted when you get there? Did you meet someone on a vacation that remained in your life? Did you go to an exotic place and sample some of their cuisine? Was there a crazy contest at a resort that you ended up entering just because? Even if you just use the places you've visited as the setting for the story, it can be a starting point for you.

There are always more ideas to be had out there, just think about your own experiences. Think about something crazy you've done. Think about people you know. Think about the drinking stories someone has told. All of these things can become plots if you just write them down.

NEWSPAPER HEADLINES

This was how *Law and Order* gets many of their ideas. They just looked in the newspaper. Steal the process from them. It's a great idea to generate those ideas that might be just out of reach, and it can make your stories feel timely.

I challenge you to turn to a random page in the paper today and just look at the headlines on the page. If one of those headlines doesn't spark a story idea, then there is something wrong with the way you think.

PLOTTING VS. PANTSING

When it comes to doing the plot of a story, there are two schools of study. There are the "Plotters" and the "Pantsers." Now, you're probably scratching your head wondering, "What the hell is he talking about?" Well, I'll let that stew in the back of your brain for a moment, but I promise that all will soon be revealed.

Best-selling author James Patterson says that before he writes a story, he pulls out a pad and writes out a summary of every scene (or chapter) and goes through it several times until he feels that he has a compelling story where the plot is moved forward in each and every scene. Only then will he actually start writing the first draft of his novel.

However, when Lee Child writes a story, he essentially has a beginning and end in mind and allows his characters to take the journey themselves. In other words, he has no more idea what's going to come next than the reader does while he's writing it.

Do you have a good idea of the difference between plotting and pantsing yet?

Plotting is where before the story even begins, the author knows what is going to happen the entire way through the novel, because they have thoroughly outlined every section of the story. Pantsing is just the opposite. There is no outline. There is no plan. The author essentially flies by the seat of his/her pants.

I have tried both, and I will tell you that both definitely work for me. For *High School Heroes*, I was definitely a pantser. I had my beginning and my end (along with a few plot points scattered about). But for the most part, I didn't know what was going to happen in the story until just I wrote it.

It's very exciting writing a story this way, because you are taking all the twists and turns with the characters, and the story can take surprising directions which can keep you motivated and passionate about it. However, this is also a way that you can write yourself into a corner, because sometimes one of those unexpected turns can very well lead into a dead-end, and the only way to backtrack is to go back and rewrite.

On the other hand, with *Anti-Christ* and *The Poe Murders*, I relied heavily on an outline. Those two books were carefully planned out to make sure that every detail I wanted, made it in. Did I make some changes as I was writing? Sure. But any writer is going to do that because as they write, fresh ideas come to mind. The important thing using this technique is that you have that roadmap to start with.

So, as an exercise I have two different outlines (on the following pages). One for the plotters and one for the pantsers. Choose which one you would rather follow and fill it out.

The Pantser Outline is for your entire novel in one shot. It isn't very detailed, but it gives you a very basic idea of where your story is going. You get to fill in the rest as you write.

The Plotter Outline is broken down by the chapter. So if you have 30 chapters in your book, you will have to fill that sheet in 30 times. Understand though, when you have a detailed outline, this is the kind of work you need to do. I promise that the work is worth it.

PANTSER CHART

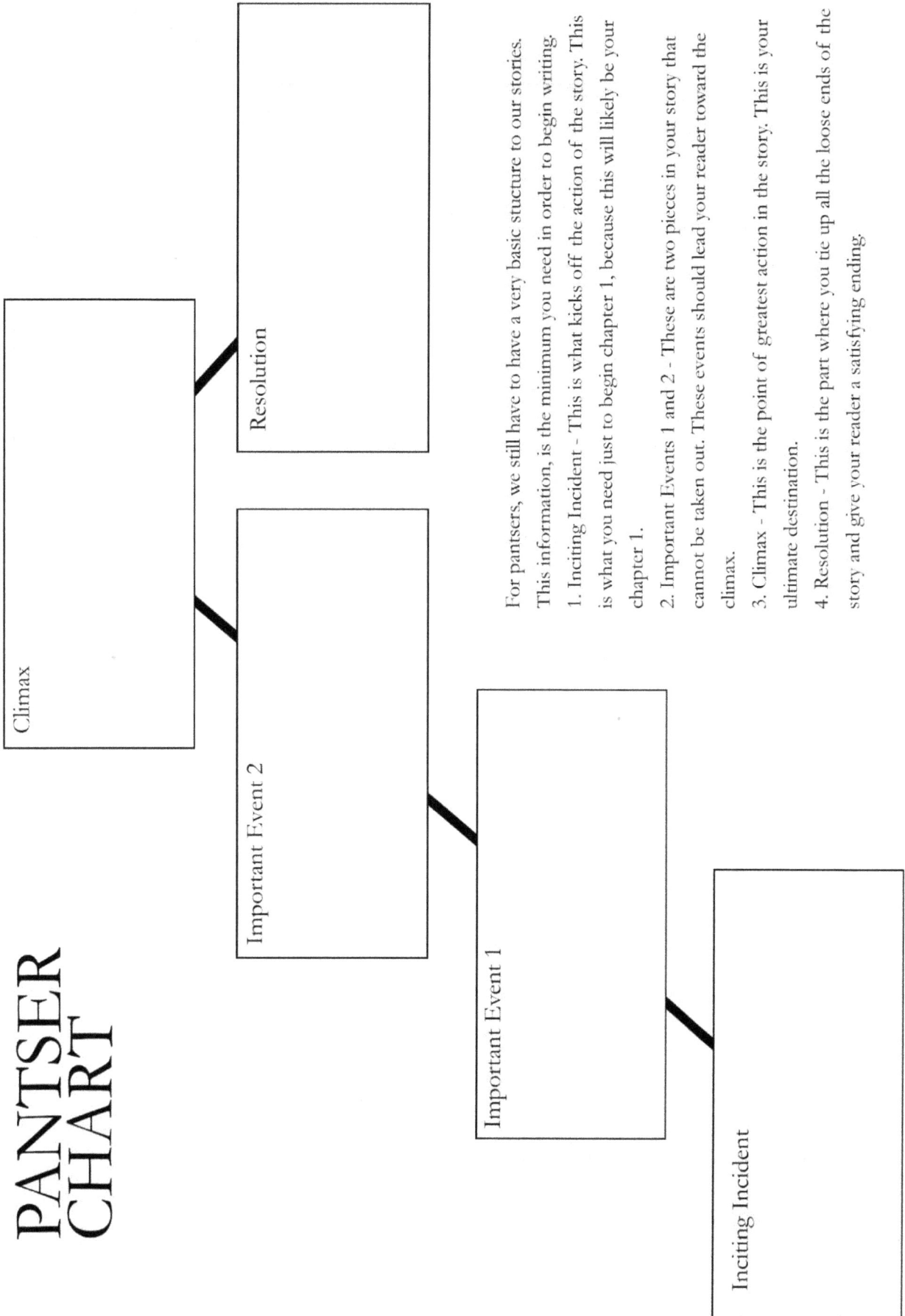

Climax

Resolution

Important Event 2

Important Event 1

Inciting Incident

For pantsers, we still have to have a very basic stucture to our stories. This information, is the minimum you need in order to begin writing

1. Inciting Incident – This is what kicks off the action of the story. This is what you need just to begin chapter 1, because this will likely be your chapter 1.

2. Important Events 1 and 2 – These are two pieces in your story that cannot be taken out. These events should lead your reader toward the climax.

3. Climax – This is the point of greatest action in the story. This is your ultimate destination.

4. Resolution – This is the part where you tie up all the loose ends of the story and give your reader a satisfying ending.

PLOTTER CHART

Chapter Number (Also Chapter Title):
Character(s) Involved in the chapter:
What are the characters trying to accomplish in this chapter?
Why are they doing it? (What is their motivation?)
What is the obstacle (or people) preventing them from accomplishing their goal?
What is at stake if they fail?
Detailed Chapter Summary:
How does this problem and goal lead to the next chapter?

Writing Prompts:

And now for the part you've all been waiting for (or skipped ahead to). Drum roll please.

Here are the writing prompts. These are the ideas to get those creative juices flowing and where you can put all that you've learned in the previous sections to good use.

There are a number of different types of prompts out there. These prompts have one sole purpose: to get the ideas flowing through your head. You can choose which ones really speak to you, or you can really challenge yourself and go down the list and try them all. When using these prompts, remember that length isn't important. You tell your story based on the prompt, when that story is done, it's done. Don't try to turn every one of these prompts into a novel—I promise, you won't be happy if you do.

In my previous book, I separated my prompts by genre. For the purposes of this book, I am not going to do that. I am going to separate them into four categories, however: Journal Prompts, Fiction Prompts, Story Starters and Picture Prompts.

Altogether, there are 200 prompts in this book. That's enough to last you for the better part of a year if you choose to do one per day.

Now for the shameless plug.

None of the prompts in this book are the same as the prompts in my previous book, *1,100 Ways To Write Your Story*. So, if you like the prompts that are here, and want even more ideas, head over to Amazon and go get this book as well.

JOURNAL PROMPTS

With journaling, you are writing about yourself. It is a way to get in touch with your past, present, and future. It's a way to jot down your ideas. These are personal, and though they can be shared, they do not have to be.

Even though I most definitely consider myself a fiction writer, I use journaling to keep ideas flowing and to keep myself in the habit of writing. I sometimes even use prompts like these to get in touch with a character in my story. Answering these prompts as if you are one of your characters is a great way to get inside his/her head.

So give it a try. You can respond to these prompts in a sentence, a paragraph, a whole essay, whatever you wish.

PROMPT 1
Write about something you used to like that you are now embarrassed by.

PROMPT 2
Write down your best sleepover memories (these can be as a kid, or as an adult).

PROMPT 3
Write about one important lesson you learned in your teens. Explain how that lesson changed who you are today.

PROMPT 4
Give advice for the next generation about how to live their lives.

PROMPT 5
Give your opinion on technology. Does it help or hinder people today?

PROMPT 6
Write about a "real life nightmare" you have experienced. What made it such a terrible ordeal?

PROMPT 7
Write about a time where you had no choice but to hurt someone. Focus on the emotions.

PROMPT 8
Write a letter to a friend you believe apologizes too much. Tell them what they need to do instead.

PROMPT 9
Give your opinion on whether it is better to save old things or throw them away.

PROMPT 10
Write about the things that clutter up your life.

PROMPT 11
Write about how you learned about sex. Think about how you changed because of it.

PROMPT 12
Give your opinion on whether you think that there are different standards for boys and girls.

PROMPT 13
Fear can be a great motivator. Write about how you use fear in your own life.

PROMPT 14
Write about how television has changed since you were a child (or teenager, or in college, or even in the last decade).

PROMPT 15
Write about a movie/television star you absolutely love and explain all the reasons why.

PROMPT 16
Write about a movie/television star you absolutely hate and explain all the reasons why.

PROMPT 17
Write a review for your favorite book as a child from a child's point of view. Then rewrite the review from your current point of view.

PROMPT 18
Write down your favorite word (or phrase) that you use every day. Then imagine that you couldn't use that word or phrase and write about what you would do or say instead.

PROMPT 19
Answer the question: Just how much information is "too much information?"

PROMPT 20
Write about your day today, but do so backwards (in other words, start with going to bed at night and end with waking up in the morning.)

PROMPT 21
Answer the question: In school, what was your favorite subject? Is it still your favorite subject today? Why or why not?

PROMPT 22
Answer the question: Do you believe that everyone has a calling in life? Why or why not?

PROMPT 23
Explain what it means to you to be "in love."

PROMPT 24
Plan an itinerary for your fantasy vacation. Then write a journal entry as if you have actually done it.

PROMPT 25
Answer the question: If you had the opportunity to go into space even if for only a few minutes, would you? Why or why not?

PROMPT 26
If you could pick another country in the world to live in, which country would it be? Explain all your reasons.

PROMPT 27
Where is your favorite place to shop? Pretend you own this store, and write about what you might do differently with it to make it even better.

PROMPT 28
Answer the question: Do you feel you get enough sleep? Why or why not?

PROMPT 29
Describe, in detail, your favorite comfort food. Use all five senses to describe it.

PROMPT 30
Describe, in detail, your least favorite food. Use all five senses to describe it.

PROMPT 31
Describe the worst vacation you have ever been on. Then, think of all the ways it could have been better and explain them.

PROMPT 32
Write down your true feelings about Valentine's Day (or another holiday if you wish).

PROMPT 33
If you could do one thing to improve the world, what would it be? Explain your choice.

PROMPT 34
Answer the question: How much do you trust the leaders in the government? Explain.

PROMPT 35
Explain how you are different now then you were ten years ago. Write about the things that have happened in that time that have caused those changes.

PROMPT 36
Answer the question: If you could outsource one task in your daily life, which one would it be? Why?

PROMPT 37
Write about how you get your news (online, newspaper, television, etc.) Now write about what you would do if that source became permanently unavailable.

PROMPT 38
Answer the question: Do you believe in ghosts? Explain.

PROMPT 39
Explain what you thought the "coolest" job was as a child. Do you feel the same way now? Explain.

PROMPT 40
Write about all the things you want to happen to you before the end of this year.

PROMPT 41
Write about the "scariest" thing you have ever eaten. Describe it using all five senses.

PROMPT 42
Write about one lesson that you have learned that you wish you could forget.

PROMPT 43
Answer the question: If you could go back to school for a new degree, and money wasn't an issue, what would you wish you could study? Explain.

PROMPT 44
Give your opinion: Classroom Learning vs. Virtual Learning (via the computer). Which is better and why? Try to think of the advantages and disadvantages of each.

PROMPT 45
Everyone is an expert at something. Write about two or three areas that you consider yourself an expert in.

PROMPT 46
Write about three things that everyone must have in order to lead a happy and successful life. Explain each of these things in detail and give examples from your own life.

PROMPT 47
Answer the question: What is the hardest part about learning a new skill?

PROMPT 48
Describe something you heard as a child that you didn't believe, but now that you are an adult you know is absolutely true.

PROMPT 49
Give your opinion: It's better to write for yourself than for other people.

PROMPT 50
Write about the moment you realized you were officially a "grown up." Write about the emotions you felt.

FICTION PROMPTS

Here is where you will find all you need for your fiction writing. These prompts (as with all the prompts in this book) can take you in any direction you choose.

There are a couple of different ways I set up these prompts. I have the story suggestion, where you are given the general idea for a story and you run with. I have the Beginning/Ending prompts, where I give you a line and you have to either start or end your story using that line. And lastly I have the word list, which is where you are given a series of related but random words, and you have to create a story using all of those words.

PROMPT 51
Write a story about someone going on a trip he/she really doesn't want to take. Think about the backstory. Think about any misadventures they may take along the way. You can choose to start the story at some random moment in the trip and fill in the details as you go.

PROMPT 52
When his/her commanding officer is found dead, one young soldier goes AWOL. Think about why this soldier does this. Think about what happens to them as a result. Get into their head as this story progresses.

PROMPT 53
Write a story about two coworkers fighting for a promotion for the same position. Think about their relationship before and after this story. Think about adding a unique conclusion.

PROMPT 54
Write a story about a man/woman who attempts to kill their spouse, but have him/her do it in a very unconventional way. In other words, he/she is not allowed to outright murder their spouse, or have someone else commit the murder either.

PROMPT 55
Write a story about a classroom that gets sealed off during a natural disaster (tornado, earthquake, etc.). Have the rescue party find them three days later. Write the story about what happens in that time.

PROMPT 56
Write a story about a witness to a murder getting coerced to join forces with the prime suspect. Think about what motivates them to take this morally ambiguous path. Think about what the rewards (or consequences) of their actions might be.

PROMPT 57
Write a story about a parent who has caught his/her child looking at material online they shouldn't be looking at.

PROMPT 58
Write a story about a man who believes girls are "prey." You can also go the other way with this and do a woman who believes the same of boys. Either way, get into the head of this person and really dive into the psychology of the story.

PROMPT 59
Write a story about college roommates, where one of them suddenly and unexpectedly finds himself/herself attracted to the other. Explore their relationship and how it changes.

PROMPT 60
While representing a known killer, an attorney falls in love with his/her client. Explore the relationship and the legal ramifications of such a thing happening.

PROMPT 61
A teenager loves to do lots of insane and wacky things. But one of thier antics has been videoed and uploaded on the internet. Now the video is going viral and the teen doesn't want everyone to see.

PROMPT 62
Humans have always wondered if they're alone in the universe. The question is finally answered when aliens arrive. But they arrive when we are fighting World War III. Write about what happens either from the alien point of view or from ours. (You could even write from both.)

PROMPT 63
A husband and wife have a "fairy tale" marriage. Everything seems perfect for them. They have good jobs, they have a nice home, and they have a baby on the way. But something occurs to cause everything to unravel quickly around them.

PROMPT 64
A CIA operative holding hundreds of classified secrets suddenly disappears. No one knows if the agent has defected, has been captured, or has been killed. Write about the hunt for this operative and the secrets he/she carries.

PROMPT 65
An airliner crashes on a deserted tropical island. Until they are rescued, the people need to learn to live off the land and with each other.

PROMPT 66
Similar to Prompt 65, but instead its a plane full of hardened criminals that were on their way to a maximum security prison.

PROMPT 67
After serving ten years for a crime he/she didn't commit, he/she gets a new identity and begins investigating the crime in order to exonerate himself/herself.

PROMPT 68
A taxi driver gets a cryptic message written on the back of dollar bill, but before he/she can question the passenger about it, they are gone.

PROMPT 69
A celebrity chef discovers a dead body on the set of his/her show. But because it would bring bad publicity, the producers want to get rid of the evidence. Explore the moral dilemma faced by the chef.

PROMPT 70

A person finds a magical mask that allows him/her to turn into anyone he wants. He/she uses this mask for his/her own nefarious purposes.

PROMPT 71
A group of teenagers spend a day having a scavenger hunt in the woods. At the end of the day, one of the teens doesn't come back. They go out to look for him/her but can find nothing.

PROMPT 72
Dreams come true for foster child who finally gets adopted. But things aren't as they seem with the child's new family and he/she begins to suspect the family might have purposely selected him/her for some dark purpose.

PROMPT 73
Write a story about a human who falls in love with an alien or magical creature.

PROMPT 74
Write a story about a person who is obsessed with the color (INSERT COLOR HERE). Write a story about he/she is instantly attracted to everything of that color, no matter where it is, or what it might be.

PROMPT 75
A babysitter snoops around her employer's house and finds a very disturbing photograph.

PROMPT 76
A character believes his/her husband/wife is cheating on him/her. He/she decides to spy on him/her and find much more than he/she was suspecting.

PROMPT 77
Explore a relationship between two people who are married, but aren't in love. Think about why they were married and write a scene in their lives.

PROMPT 78
On campus, a student discovers another group of students sneaking around to meet secretly at regular intervals. The student decides one night to follow them and gets the shock of his/her life.

PROMPT 79
A young boy/girl is sent to an orphanage after his/her parents are killed. The orphanage, while nice on the outside, is run like an animal shelter on the inside.

PROMPT 80
A character wakes up one morning and finds himself/herself tied to the bed and gagged. Sitting in a chair next to the bed is someone the person knows. Explore the situation.

PROMPT 81
A man/woman contacts a long lost child he/she had given up years before. After contact, his/her world gets turned upside down.

PROMPT 82
A man/woman opens up a fortune cookie with the following message. "Your life is in danger. Say

nothing to anyone. Leave immediately." What happens next?

PROMPT 83
A man/woman begins receiving flowers and gifts from an anonymous source. His/her husband/wife begins to grow suspicious even though he/she has done nothing wrong. Then the gifts begin to get strange.

PROMPT 84
A young teen gets caught shoplifting. The manager of the store says he/she won't call the police as long as the teen does him/her a personal favor.

PROMPT 85
A man/woman is blamed for a murder they cannot remember committing, though every piece of evidence points to them. Explore the psychological profile of this person as you write your story.

PROMPT 86
Write a story about your protagonist having horrific nightmares. Then, have the nightmares begin to affect his/her daily life to the point they can no longer distinguish dream from reality.

PROMPT 87
Write a story about a man/woman experiencing their mid-life crisis and deciding to go sky-diving for the first time. Everyone thinks this is strange, since the man/woman is deathly afraid of heights.

PROMPT 88
A man/woman has a boyfriend/girlfriend of another race (White, Black, Hispanic, etc.) He/she has to bring this person to meet his/her parents. But his/her father is a member of the KKK. Write the scene right before they walk into the house to the point where they meet with the father.

PROMPT 89
A man/woman believes that his/her boss is looking for any excuse to fire him/her. Instead of trying to do his/her job as best as possible, he/she decides to fight back.

PROMPT 90
Write a story about a couple who go out on a date, and who both find themselves attracted to the waiter/waitress, but don't want to let their partner know. Write the story from both points of view.

PROMPT 91
Scientists have found a radio frequency that the dead communicate in. They figure out a way to tap into that frequency. Write a story that explores the repercussions.

PROMPT 92
While on vacation, a man/woman finds a book that is eerily like his/her own life. The further they read the more like him/her it becomes. He/she reads to the end and believes they now know their own future, and is not sure whether or not he/she likes it.

PROMPT 93
Write a story about a pyromaniac whose greatest fear is being burned alive.

PROMPT 94

Write a story about a kids' sleepover that doesn't go as planned.

PROMPT 95
A man/woman decides to take his/her day off and go to the (INSERT LOCATION HERE). While there, they see someone who could easily be their identical twin. This other person sees them and runs toward them angrily.

PROMPT 96
Create a world in which politicians are required to wear the logos of all their financial supporters (think NASCAR). Write a story that would show one of these politicians.

PROMPT 97
A man/woman walks to work one morning, only to be delayed by a large group of people dancing naked in the streets. When he/she gets to work, his/her boss does not believe the excuse.

PROMPT 98
Write a story about a person who can control people by touching their shadows.

PROMPT 99
A man/woman is in a horrible car accident and is in a coma for several months. What his/her family, doctors and nurses don't realizes is that he/she can hear every word they say. When he/she wakes up, he/she has a lot of decisions to make.

PROMPT 100
Write a story from several different points of view. The setting: The last day before the world explodes.

STORY STARTERS

For the next 50 prompts, begin your story with the words in the prompt. Then you can take that prompt in any direction you choose.

Using these prompts should give your story a very compelling opening that will grip your reader from the beginning. Don't hold back, let your imagination run wild. Come up with something great. Also, remember, these can be short stories, flash fiction, or a full-length work.

PROMPT 101
He/she wasn't at all what I was expecting…

PROMPT 102
They would never be able to cover up the smell of the body from the officer…

PROMPT 103
He/she was a wonderful liar…

PROMPT 104
He/she hurled the phone up against the wall…

PROMPT 105
He/she rolled over and pushed up against something hard…

PROMPT 106
My husband/wife disappeared six years ago today…

PROMPT 107
Every morning the sun came up and every night it went down again. Until…

PROMPT 108
It took a year to discover my fortuneteller was mistaken…

PROMPT 109
It might have looked like a present, but it was really…

PROMPT 110
He/she couldn't believe it had come to this…

PROMPT 111
"It's not what you think!" he/she screamed…

PROMPT 112
I stared at the sign trying to figure out what Y.O.P.R. stood for...

PROMPT 113

Their plea went unheard…

PROMPT 114
He/she jumped up onto the ledge…

PROMPT 115
"I just cleaned all those uniforms!" he/she shouted…

PROMPT 116
He/she never thought he/she would drink paint, but…

PROMPT 117
He/she was fifteen minutes late, and the entire place was empty…

PROMPT 118
"Let's go somewhere," he/she whispered…

PROMPT 119
"You really should have enjoyed your first year here," he/she said…

PROMPT 120
I always hated my commander…

PROMPT 121
The attack was over in seconds…

PROMPT 122
The most vivid memory he/she had of his/her hometown was…

PROMPT 123
"Are you seriously telling me you lost the lottery ticket?"

PROMPT 124
It was a most unusual pregnancy, ending in a most unusual birth…

PROMPT 125
This morning, I got a phone call that ruined my whole day…

PROMPT 126
Some jokes just aren't funny…

PROMPT 127
The floorboard creaked, filling me with fear…

PROMPT 128
The snow just wouldn't stop falling…

PROMPT 129
"Don't you dare wish me a Happy New Year!" he/she yelled…

PROMPT 130
The number 17 has always had a special meaning for me...

PROMPT 131
The minister leaned over the podium and pointed a finger directly at him/her...

PROMPT 132
Low battery. The two words I definitely didn't need to see right now...

PROMPT 133
That car was so sexy...

PROMPT 134
He/she couldn't believe his/her best friend was a ghost...

PROMPT 135
Something moved in the pantry...

PROMPT 136
Normally, he/she wouldn't go out on a night like this, but...

PROMPT 137
He/she had enjoyed a decade of being completely irresponsible...

PROMPT 138
The wind had never blown like this before...

PROMPT 139
I had nothing left but pride...

PROMPT 140
The jewels sparkled in the beam of sunlight...

PROMPT 141
How can someone get lost twice in one day?

PROMPT 142
He/she knew his coworker shouldn't have been fired, but if he'd said something...

PROMPT 143
"You are a very clever girl"...

PROMPT 144
Half the names on the list had already been crossed off...

PROMPT 145
Only the desperate need apply...

PROMPT 146
I couldn't remember who had talked me into this…

PROMPT 147
He/she refused to let them see him/her cry…

PROMPT 148
Just a few more steps, and…

PROMPT 149
The money hadn't been worth stealing…

PROMPT 150
The limo stopped and the tinted windows rolled down to reveal…

PROMPT 151
Never judge a stripper by her glitter…

PROMPT 152
The sign read "No Trespassing"…

PROMPT 153
Three days from now, I'll be dead…

PROMPT 154
"Sit down, or else," he shouted…

PROMPT 155
It was too damned quiet…

PROMPT 156
This is why you should never lend a friend money…

PROMPT 157
When you get hungry enough…

PROMPT 158
The sponge sat on the table between them…

PROMPT 159
The boy/girl hid under the table…

PROMPT 160
Never make me angry…

WORTH 1,000 WORDS

This is pretty simple. I have 40 images. All you have to do is take the image and tell the story behind it. You can do the backstory that leads up to what happens in the picture, you can tell what is happening in the picture, or you can use the picture as the starting off point of your story.

I would like to extend a challenge to you on this one. I know earlier I said that length didn't matter, but my challenge to you is this. For each picture you choose to write about, try and write at least 1,000 words for it, hence the title of this section.

Before you go to the actual pictures, I would just like to note that all of these images are in the public domain, and I downloaded them from the following websites: publicdomainpictures.net, unsplash.com, defense.gov, and pixabay.com.

Image 1

Image 2

Image 3

Image 4

Image 5

Image 6

Image 7

Image 8

Image 9

Image 10

Image 11

Image 12

Image 13

Image 14

Image 15

Image 16

Image 17

Image 18

Image 19

Image 20

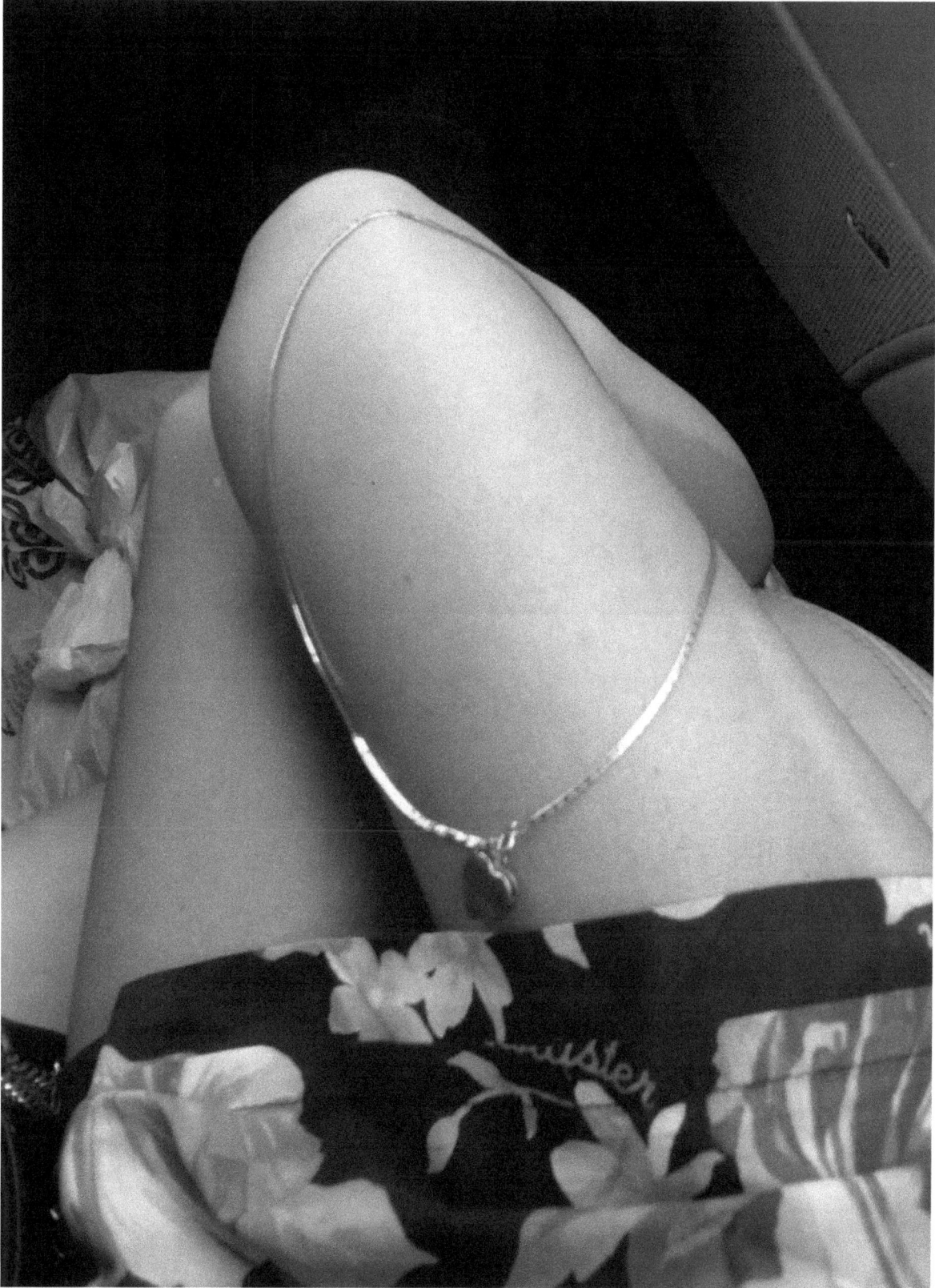

Image 21

Image 22

Image 23

Image 24

Image 25

Image 26

Image 27

Image 28

Image 29

Image 30

Image 31

Image 32

Image 33

Image 34

Image 35

Image 36

Image 37

Image 38

Image 39

Image 40

I've Written My Book…
Now What?

It's a perfectly logical question to ask. Most books will tell you how to write a story and give you thousands of tips and tricks for how to do that, but they won't go further than that. I, on the other hand, will.

As I've told you before, I have gotten my books traditionally published as well as self-publishing them. So, I have experienced both sides. Which one is better? That is completely up to your own personal preference. I am not going to tell you one way or the other what you should go for. I will, however, map out the pros and cons and give you some helpful hints for both.

Understand that whether you go the traditional route and get yourself a publisher, or if you decide to go it on your own and self-publish, you are going to be doing a good amount of legwork to get your book seen. Gone are the days where you can publish something and then not promote it, hoping that that word of mouth is going to be enough to get you noticed. So, we will have a section for that too.

I will walk you through finding and using an editor, as well as getting yourself a good cover (because as we all know people DO judge books by their covers).

Now that everything has been written, the hard work can begin.

GOING THE TRADITIONAL ROUTE

Many people prefer this way. They feel that there is more prestige by getting picked up by a big publisher. They feel like it will be less work on their part if they can get themselves signed with a big publisher. Their books will get into bookstores and be more likely to reach the *New York Times Bestseller List*.

For the most part, they're right. There is more prestige with the big publishers (at least it looks better when you try and publish another book). You will have less legwork at the beginning when trying to get your book out. And you are more likely to get your book into bookstores and thus onto a bestseller list.

That's not to say you can't get your book into stores or make it a bestseller by self-publishing, but it is more of a challenge.

AGENTS

If you are going to try for the traditional route, you are more than likely going to need an agent. Now, like any group of people, there are some good agents, and there are some bad ones. The bad ones will never sell your book and they make money off of you, the author. An agent is supposed to make money from the publisher, taking a small percentage (usually around 20% of your royalties) when you get published. A bad agent is going to charge the author upfront for their services (plus a percentage of the royalties), and is likely not going to get you in anywhere you couldn't have gotten into by yourself (see the EDITORS section). These people aren't reputable, and if you look at their client list, you wouldn't see any recognizable names or books.

There is a website called Preditors & Editors (https://www.pred-ed.com) that will help you distinguish the good from the bad. Before sending in your stuff anywhere, I would suggest looking at this site.

An agent is going to want to see a proposal package (See PROPOSALS section). Before you submit anything to an agent, make sure you have everything they are asking for. Also, before you send to an agent, your book has to be completed. They do not want to see half-finished projects. So if you have not yet finished your writing, you really shouldn't bother moving on until you have.

EDITORS

An agent will usually get you in front of an editor at the publishing houses. However, there is always the possibility of skipping the middle-man and getting your work directly in front of an editor. There are some publishers that will simply accept proposals from an author, though most of them won't. If you do your research you will be able to find them.

Even the editors from the big publishers, who won't even look in your direction unless you have an agent, will take proposals from a select group of un-agented writers. If you attend a conference or a workshop that the editor (or their publisher) is hosting or attending, they will usually be given the opportunity to submit to them without going through an agent. The window on this is usually limited (say within a month of the conference), but it does afford an opportunity. So if you attend such writing conferences, this is something you might want to look into.

Much of what I said for an agent is true of these editors. Look to the Preditors & Editors website, and make sure before you send anything, that you have a solid proposal ready.

FINDING AGENTS & EDITORS

So, that's what agents and editors are all about, but what do you do to find them. I do not suggest a Google search. Most reputable agents won't be found that way. I have two resources that I use when looking for agents and editors. Both of them are pretty accurate, and they are both updated at least once a year.

To be honest, I recommend you use both resources for submitting your proposals.

Everyone Who's Anyone – https://www.everyonewhosanyone.com
This is a website run by Gerard Jones, an author who was tired of slogging through hundreds of sites to find information on editors and agents. So, he created a database of nearly every English speaking agent and editor in the world. Most of them are in the United States, but he does also cover Canada and Britain. He even has special sections for magazine and newspaper editors, as well as movie studios and Hollywood agents. So, if you are looking for an agent or an editor, this is the site to look at.

The downside to this site is, though it does list all contact information for each of these people in the publishing industry, it doesn't tell you what they publish, or the types of books they represent. So, this site will take a bit of extra research on your part.

Writer's Digest – Writer's Market – https://www.writersmarket.com
While this is another online database of agents and editors (though not quite as far reaching as Everyone Who's Anyone), I prefer the physical book. While Everyone Who's Anyone is a free site, this one is not. It will cost you about the same for the book as it does for a year of online access (and if you buy the book, you get the online access anyway).

Though it isn't free, this site does let you know what each person wants to see, including how to submit your proposal. So, the information you are going to gain here will be invaluable.

LOGLINE

Before I get to your proposal, it is important to have your logline. This is a brief, one-sentence, summary of what your story is about. This is not only your selling point to potential agents and editors, but it can be your pitch to potential customers as well.

A logline has to summarize the whole story, be catchy, and make people want to learn more about your story.

For example, my logline for *The Poe Murders*, is as follows:

"It takes all the old Edgar Allan Poe stories and meshes them together as if they are happening in the same place, at the same time, in one big murder mystery."

Admittedly, this is a mouthful, but I have practiced it so much that I can spout it out in a couple seconds and get someone to take a look at the book. You need to create something similar.

Here is the one I use for *Anti-Christ*:

"A young woman, on the run from a terrorist cell that believes her to be the spawn of Satan with the power to wipe out the Western World, fights to use her powers for good only to discover she really is a monster."

Again, if you look, it's my entire story summed up into one sentence, and hopefully it gets you to want to know more about the story.

Here are a couple of examples from movies:

The Shawshank Redemption-Two imprisoned men bond over a number of years, finding solace and eventual redemption through acts of common decency.

The Hangover–A Las Vegas comedy centered around three groomsmen who lose their about-to-be-wed buddy during their drunken misadventures, then must retrace their steps in order to find him.

Titanic –A young man and woman from different social classes fall in love aboard an ill-fated voyage at sea.

Hopefully you get the idea. If not, you can always look up some more examples online. The point is, that before you begin your proposal, have this handy.

So, get to work on creating that kick-ass logline.

PROPOSALS

You've seen this word a couple of times over the last few pages. If you are going the traditional route in publishing, this is probably the most important piece to get you there. Now, I wish I could say this was easy, but frankly that would be a lie. The proposal is probably the hardest part of the entire process for me. I know other authors that do not feel the same way, but for a creative person like me, the part of trying to "sell" my book to an agent or publisher is very difficult.

The worst part is, while there is some basic information that every proposal must have, every agent and editor is different and all want different things. Some want to see it as an email, some still want to see it come by regular (snail) mail. Some want to see the first three chapters, some want to see the first 10 pages, some don't want to see anything at all. Some want books between 70,000 and 100,000 words, others don't want to see anything over 50,000 words. That is why the resources in the previous section are invaluable, because they will help spell out for you what each and every one of them wants.

What All Proposals Must Have

The list of "musts" for a proposal is notoriously short.

1. Query letter.
2. Query letter.
3. Query letter.

There is no proposal without one of these. It doesn't matter if you've written a children's book or if you've written the next *War and Peace*. You must have a query letter. No matter what any agent or editor asks for, this is the must. There are some that will only want you to send this.

If you are new to writing, the best way to describe a query letter is that it is almost like a cover letter. The only difference is that instead of convincing someone you are the right person for a job, this is to convince them to represent or publish your book.

This piece is probably the most important, mainly because no matter if they are asking for just this letter or an entire package, this is the first thing they are going to look at. So, first and foremost, this is a writing sample, for these agents and editors to see your writing ability. If you send them a letter that is fraught with misspellings and grammatical errors, they aren't even going to bother reading anything else.

It is also a place for you to outline your story in a compelling way. Think of it as writing the summary for the back cover of the book. Something that is going to intrigue the reader and make them want to read more.

A query letter needs to only be a few short paragraphs.

Paragraph 1

The first is your logline. This is going to hook your reader (hopefully).

Paragraph 2

Next, is a short paragraph further summarizing the story. Make it no more than four to five sentences.

Paragraph 3

Third paragraph is the "technical" aspects of the book. You give the reader the full title, the length, the genre and the audience. You can also include in this paragraph books or movies that your story is like. However, avoiding saying things like, "This is the next Harry Potter." Agents and editors hate that.

Paragraph 4

This is where you talk about yourself. You tell anything that is pertinent to the telling of the story, and include any publishing credits you have (if any). For instance, if you're writing a book on education and you've been a teacher for 20 years, that's where this will go. If you are writing a sci-fi novel and did extensive research on technology that you used in it, include that here. I usually write this paragraph in the third-person.

Paragraph 5

Just a simple thank you.

Do not write more than this. Your cover letter should ideally be no longer than three-quarters of a page. Any more than that and it is likely not going to be read (or at least not all the way through). On the flip-side, if you have less than a half-page when all is said and done, that is too short.

All other rules for a typical business-type letter apply to the cover letter as well. You want your name and contact information to appear at the top, followed by the name and contact information of the person you are sending it to. You want to include a "Sincerely" at the end, as well as a signature (if you are sending by regular mail).

On the following page I have an example from *Anti-Christ*:

James Mascia
Address
City, State, Zip Code
Phone
Email

Editor Name
Address
City, State, Zip Code
Phone
Email

Dear _____,

A young woman, on the run from a terrorist cell that believes her to be the spawn of Satan with the power to wipe out the Western World, fights to use her powers for good only to discover she really is a monster.

What if you were created to be the ultimate evil in the world and didn't want to be? What if you were the monster in your own horror movie? What would you do? These are questions Sam asks herself every day. She has a dark power within her that hurts all those she comes near. Wishing to rid herself of this power she turns to the only option she believes will work—suicide. But after several attempts, she realizes that she is not allowed to die. Sam is soon caught in a world where she is being chased down by supernatural beings, Satanic-cults, and terrorist groups, all believing that she has the power to destroy the world. When she is pushed too far, she decides to fight back, only to make matters worse. Try as she might, she can't use her dark powers to help or save anyone, not even herself, and the more she uses them the closer she brings the world to the brink of annihilation.

Anti-Christ is a 73,000 word thriller which tests the idea that the Anti-Christ is a being of pure evil. It will allow the reader to get inside the head of the monster while rooting for her to beat back the darkness.

James Mascia is the author of several novels and graphic novels including *High School Heroes* and *The Poe Murders* which have each sold more than 15,000 copies. He is an English and Writing teacher at both the high school and college levels.

Thank you for your consideration. I look forward to hearing from you.

Sincerely,

James Mascia
Email Again

Synopsis

Accompanying the cover letter should be a short synopsis. This is a detailed summary of your book that is no longer than one page.

With the synopsis, you want to leave no mystery for the reader. The agents and editors want to know that you have a compelling ending for your story, so they don't want you to write a synopsis that includes everything up to the climax and then asks them a question. I know that as a writer this is our natural inclination, but it isn't something you want to do. Tell the ending, let them know exactly what is going to happen. If you have a good enough ending, they will want to know more about your story.

This part may be asked for, but it may not be. It all depends on the person you're sending it to.

Here is an example. Once again, it is from my proposal for *Anti-Christ*.

SYNOPSIS

Sam wants out.

She has a dark power inside her she neither understands, nor wants, and everyone and everything she touches falls to ruin before her eyes.

But try as she might to commit suicide, something always intercedes and prevents her from dying. She can't figure out why until she discovers the Devil himself has been her rescuer. And he has plans for her.

Things become clearer as Sam is picked up by a terrorist cell operating within the United States. She learns that she has been bred with the sole purpose of destroying the Western World. They have created her with help from supernatural forces much the same way God created Jesus Christ, and they expect her to fulfill her destiny. But like everyone else who gets close to her, the terrorists who have kidnapped her fall to a horrific fate.

Now, hunted by forces both physical and supernatural, Sam must decide—if she truly cannot die, does she run and hide from her fate, or does she fulfill her destiny as the Anti-Christ? She cannot see herself bringing about the end of the world, but she does not believe she is going to be given any other choice.

Sam fights to escape Satanic cults, terrorist cells and demons, even as she learns more about her own power and where she came from. She decides that she is going to prevent her fate by using her power on the very people who created her. But in doing, so she will bring about the events chronicled in the Book of Revelation, and she must watch as the world around her is destroyed. Only then will the Devil allow her to die.

Story Sample

Yes, we finally get to the sample of your story.

Agents and editors want to see the beginning of your story as a sample. I have seen them ask for only the first page, the first chapter, the first ten pages, the first three chapters, etc. Essentially, they can ask you for just about any amount of the book starting from the beginning.

You must be sure that these pages you send in are absolutely perfect. So, you should go through it with a fine-tooth comb, and have someone else do it too. Even when I send my books out for traditional publication, I have an editor look at them first. Yes, it's true that if you get picked up by a publisher, they are going to have an editor go through your book. However, if you are still an unpublished author, you want to make the greatest impression possible with your manuscript, which means that you should have it edited prior to sending it anywhere. (For further info on Professional Editors, see the section under Going it Alone.)

As far as formatting goes, you want to have your manuscript in Times New Roman (or like font) at 12 point and have the manuscript double-spaced. (A note on double-spacing: don't go through your entire manuscript and hit <ENTER> at the beginning of every line to give yourself some extra space. There is a setting in most word processors that will allow you to double space the entire document with a couple clicks of the mouse. Doing it by hitting <ENTER> will show on the document when you send it and it reeks of unprofessionalism.) This is the standard format for manuscripts. It isn't the only format. Check with each agent or editor and see what their specifications are. If they have no specifications, assume that it is what I listed above.

Writing Resume

I have never actually sent this out, but I have noticed that agents and editors do sometimes ask for this. All they are looking for is a list of your previous publications (if any). As long as you include this information in your cover letter, you should be fine.

GOING IT ALONE

For some of us, we don't want to go through the tedious process of sending out query letter after query letter and continue getting rejections (or no response at all) for months on end. If this doesn't sound like something you are willing to do, then self-publishing is probably for you.

Understand before you get into self-publishing, you can't just publish a book and expect it to sell. Remember that self-publishing effectively means that you are now the book's publisher, which means that you are now responsible for all the duties that would have been performed by a regular book publisher—editing, designing, promoting, selling. All of these things now completely fall into your lap. So, if you are thinking of taking the self-publishing route, remember that it will be hard work.

RULE NUMBER ONE

The first thing I want to tell you about self-publishing is that is should never cost you money to publish your book. There are plenty of publishers out there who will charge you just to publish your book through them, and then they also charge you to purchase your own book from them. In other words, these publishers are making money on YOU, the author, when they should be making money off your customers.

We call these vanity publishers, and the top two that come to mind are iUniverse and Publish America. I have experience with both. Back when I was still a fledgling college student, I fell for these publishers. After all, they were going to publish my book, they were going to format it, and get me a great cover (the covers weren't all that great either). But at the time, it was the only way you could self-publish.

As I said, don't fall into the trap of paying a publisher to publish. This is not something you want to do, especially considering that some of these packages can run you upwards of $1,000 or more (and that doesn't even include editing or marketing your book. If you want those additions, it is a sizeable cost to upgrade). Then they charge you $15 per book. So to order just 10 books, you need to shell out $150, plus shipping costs. In order to make even the tiniest profit on these books, you need to charge at least $20 (it comes to about a $2.50 profit when all is said and done). And let me tell you there are not many people out there who are willing to pay $20 for a book from an author they have never heard of.

Now, it's true, that to do it yourself, you will have to spend money, but nowhere near what it costs for one of these places. And the money you spend will be for the development of the book, not a publisher to publish it. The money you spend should be investing in yourself, and if you do it right, it will cost you a lot less than $1,000 and you will have a book that you will be able sell.

In this section, I am going to show you how you can self-publish your book, for a fraction of what it would cost you to go to one of those vanity publishers. Starting with where you should publish both Ebooks and Print Books (yes, you will have to do it separately).

CREATESPACE

This is the best place to go for printing your books. If you don't know, this site is run by Amazon. The best part is, it's absolutely free. The only cost to you is the cost of printing your book. If you remember, I told you a book at those vanity presses will cost you $15, plus shipping. Well, at Createspace, I print my books (with shipping) for around $5, depending on the size of the book. I then sell them for $10, and make about a $5 profit. And because the book is cheaper, I also sell more of them, so it is a win/win all around.

And I know, wow, I'm actually telling you how much I pay for my own books and how much profit I make, a usual "no no." But, I am giving you every piece of information I have available, I am literally (and pardon the pun) an open book.

The other reason I like Createspace is that it is easy to upload your book, and they also have a free 24 hour customer support line if you have any issues. They even have articles on their website with subject like formatting your book, and marketing that are well worth the read.

The important thing to remember is that when you do choose to upload your book, make sure it is in PDF format. The PDF format is the only way to ensure that what goes on the page is EXACTLY the way you have the book set up.

You can make a PDF straight from Microsoft Word, just by choosing "Save As" and selecting PDF for the file format. I cannot speak for any of the other word processing software, but I would assume that some of them have a similar function.

Createspace requires an ISBN in order to publish with them. You can get a free ISBN through them, however, if you do so Createspace will be listed as the publisher. You can also purchase one for about $10, if you want to be listed as the publisher.

Createspace does have some optional extras, for those of you who feel that you need them, you may consider them, but I don't really recommend them because the price is so high. You can have them professionally edit your book, have your book cover designed, market your book, amongst other things. The only thing I might recommend (if you feel you cannot do it yourself) is the Layout and Design extra. The cheapest option is currently $149 (which, while there are cheaper options out there, you probably won't get as good quality). But for this, you will get your book professionally formatted so that it appears perfect inside and you won't run into any printing problems. However, I will add, that this is pretty easy to do, and you should be able to do it with little problem.

Createspace also has a cover designer program on the site, which I also do not recommend, because the premade covers in their database there are very basic. Look at my section on book covers for more info on why you don't want that.

Anyway, the best advice I can give you for Createspace is to get on the site, and play around with it. The book won't be officially published until you hit that publish button. Until you do, you can keep making changes to the book.

EBOOKS

Creating an ebook is probably easier than doing it for print (which is why there are so many more ebooks out there than print books). The best thing about the ebooks is, if you are able to do it yourself, there is absolutely no cost. You don't have to pay for copies of the book. You don't have to pay to post it on any sites. All you have to do is post it.

Believe it or not, an ebook actually requires less formatting than a print book. Yes, there are certain things you must do, like making sure you aren't using any freaky fonts, and if you have images, they can be a pain to work with. Otherwise, formatting an ebook is pretty easy. Like mentioned before, if you cannot do it yourself, there are services out there that can format them for you.

There are a number of sites out there you can post to. But I have found two that work the best. They are Kindle Direct Publishing and Smashwords.

Kindle Direct Publishing
https://kdp.amazon.com/
Kindle is easily the biggest powerhouse in the ebook market (yes, sorry iPad users, but it's true.) While that might change one day, the one device you want to make sure you get your ebook onto is the Kindle. The ONLY way to do that is through Kindle Direct Publishing (KDP).

They have a pretty easy interface for uploading your ebook. They ask you a bunch of information, and then ask you to upload your book. Now, the book must be formatted properly to their standards before they will accept it for publication. So, make sure your book is presentable. If the book is an absolute disgrace, they will tell you to try again.

To publish for Kindle you do not need an ISBN number (more on that later), but there are ways to get yourself one for free.

Like Createspace, this site is run by Amazon, and it is very easy to use. Unfortunately, unlike Createspace, it is not as customer service friendly, which means that if you have a question, you are largely on your own, unless you wish to wait 48 hours for a response to a comment on their contact form (and they don't make the form easy to find either).

Generally, once you submit a book to KDP, it takes them less than 12 hours before it is live on Amazon—in other words, if you submit your book at 8 a.m., and there are no problems that are flagged by Amazon, your ebook will be available for sale by 8 p.m. the same day.

Kindle Select
Now, KDP has a program called Kindle Select. Which is a service kind of like Netflix, but for books. Essentially, anyone who pays for the Kindle Select service, which is only $10 per month, they can download any book and read it for free that is in the Kindle Select program. The author gets paid a fee based on how many pages they read of that book. So, if someone reads 15 pages of your book you might make 10 cents, but if someone reads 150 pages, you'd get $1 (I'm generalizing, that is likely not how much you'd make). The numbers change every month based on the "fund" they have for the program (I guess it depends on how many people are signed up for it that month or something, I'm not really sure how it works), and it gets divided amongst the authors.

The caveat for having your book in this program, however, is that you must publish exclusively on Kindle. This can be good or bad and it's a decision you will have to make when you publish your ebook. By having your book for free with this program, you will be able to attract new readers that might not otherwise give your book a second glance. You can get reviews for it more easily (reviews are a good thing). And you can tap into that fund where you will get a small percentage of money for every page that gets read of your book in any given month. Plus, your book will be available on the biggest ebook seller's site.

On the other hand, your book will ONLY be on the biggest ebook seller's site, and you will not be able to publish it anywhere else, which means that you could lose sales from iTunes, Kobo, Nook, etc.

It is a tough decision, but you have to decide which best benefits you and your book. Are you more likely to make money just selling on Amazon? Or do you think that you will get more books sold selling them all over the internet? That is a question I cannot answer for you. I will tell you that there are some books of mine that are in the Kindle Select program. There are also books of mine that will NEVER be in the Kindle Select program, including this one.

You can always give it a try if you're not sure. But understand this, that once you sign up for Kindle Select, you are obligated to have it exclusive on Kindle for three months. Again, the choice is yours.

SMASHWORDS
https://www.smashwords.com

The other site I use for ebooks is Smashwords. I was reluctant of this site at first, and tentatively only published one book on it just to try it. Almost three years later and I have almost twenty ebooks on their site, including this one. I was reluctant because it was a company I had never heard of before, and the idea that THEY would distribute my book sounded sketchy to me. However, it has been a blessing.

Smashwords publishes to virtually every ebook site you've ever heard of (and some you probably haven't). They get your books onto the Baker and Taylor site, which distributes to libraries. They are also probably the easiest way to get your book listed in the iTunes (or iBooks) store, which makes you downloadable on iPads and iPhones without having the Kindle app. As a matter of fact, the only place they don't publish you is on Kindle (so you can't get on Amazon with this site). They say they will publish you on Amazon, however if you read the fine print, you need to sell something absurd like 10,000 of a single title before that title is eligible for distribution to Amazon. Since most of us aren't going to achieve that, it's a safe bet to say you won't be making it on Amazon through Smashwords.

Smashwords requires an ISBN in order to publish with them (or at least for them to distribute you). You can get a free ISBN through them, however, if you do so Smashwords will be listed as the publisher, much like Createspace was for print. This really doesn't make much of a difference, unless you would like to be listed as a publisher, in which case you will want to pay for an ISBN, which you can also do through their site (the cost is $10). I usually go for the free one, since I haven't really noticed any effect on sales when I've paid for the ISBN vs. getting it free.

What I usually do with books, however, is I get my free ISBN for the ebook through this site, and then put that ISBN on the book when I publish it through Amazon. There is nothing wrong with doing this, all it is doing is tracking the book and sales through some database. Once the ISBN is assigned to your book, it belongs only to that book, no matter where it is published.

EDITING

I mentioned editing briefly in the traditional publishing section, but now I am going to go into a lot more detail, even giving you some places where you can get your book edited.

Like I mentioned earlier, no matter where you are sending this, or what you're doing with it, you need to have an editor. An editor is going to, at the very least, go through your manuscript with a fine tooth comb and pull out all the errors in it. For those of you who think you can do it yourself, I want to dissuade you.

I am a pretty decent editor. At school, I edit and pick apart my students' essays and other writings. I can spot run-on sentences a mile away. I know the differences of "they're," "there" and "their" and the proper times to use each. But I still don't trust myself to edit my own manuscripts—at least, not by myself.

To be sure, I will go through my manuscript and edit it before I give it to someone to edit. Usually, it will go through several rounds of edits, just to make sure that everything is caught. I will edit the manuscript as I am going through and revising for my second and third drafts. I will then go through it again after I am done with the manuscript. Then, I will send it out to an editor and have him or her go through it. Then, after I have fixed all the edits the editor has made, I will go through it one last time.

By the end of this process, I will pretty much be able to tell you where you can find every word and phrase is in the book. That's okay. I like having intimate knowledge of my books.

This is the point I will either self-publish it, or start sending it out to agents and editors.

Here is the problem though: the cost. There is no way you are going to get this done without spending at least a few hundred dollars (unless you have a really short book). For a 50,000 word novel, which is still a short novel, you're looking at a minimum of $500 for *quality* editing. Most editing services will cost more.

Now, you will notice I emphasized the word *quality* in that last sentence. That's because you can find cheaper options out there, but these options will likely leave your manuscript in no better condition than when you started. Yes, changes will be made, but maybe not the right ones. If you feel confident enough to still go with one of these options, I'm not going to stop you (not that I could anyway). However, the places I am going to list here, are going to be for the quality editing I mentioned.

As usual, there are others. I would check that Preditors and Editors website I mentioned earlier (https://www.pred-ed.com). This will also have a review of several other editing services (as well as which ones to avoid).

I have either used these editing services, or I know an author who has. Either way, these are decent ones to start with.

Shelley's Editing Service – https://www.shelleyseditingservice.com

New York Book Editors – https://www.nybookeditors.com

Adian Editing – https://www.adianediting.com

Novel Doctor – https://www.noveldoctor.com

What to Expect

Mostly we now send our manuscripts to editors electronically. They will want to have it in some form of Microsoft Word format (mostly). This is the easiest for them to edit on. Some editors will want the physical copy, and you will have to send it to them through the regular mail. They will mark it up with a red pen, just like the English teachers of olden days would do. They will go through it and they will make changes. This can take a few days to a few weeks, depending on the editor (and their current workload).

When you get the manuscript back, it isn't done yet. Whether you gave it to them electronically or not, you will still have to make changes. Essentially, the editor will go through and make changes, but the changes won't be final on the manuscript until you approve them. You do reserve the right to reject any changes the editor makes to the manuscript (and yes, even the professional editors can make mistakes, so don't blindly accept them all). Most editors will also answer questions you have about any changes they've made, so they can explain it to you if you're confused why they added or deleted something.

After you've gone through it and looked at the changes, it is usually done. I have known some editors who will take a second look through it, just to double-check everything, but not all editors will do this.

Only after you are both satisfied with the changes, should you consider the book ready for sending out or publishing.

JUDGE A BOOK BY ITS COVER

Judging a book by its cover—something that we are never supposed to do. But it is something we all do. It is sad to say, but a bad cover can kill your book.

I can certainly attest to this fact. When *High School Heroes* was originally published, it had the most god-awful cover I think I have ever seen. It was a point in which I argued with my publisher on over and over again for a year. Unfortunately, since that publisher still holds the copyright on the cover, I am unable to show it to you. However, it can still be found in some dark corners of the internet if you look hard enough.

Besides having an awful image, the cover of the book also misrepresented what was inside. The book is a superhero book, but my publisher decided to put a football player front and center. So when people saw the title, *High School Heroes,* and then the football player, they assumed it was a sports book (as well they should). The disappointment when they discovered what it was really about, paired with the fact that it looked like a fifth grader created the cover, I was unable to sell it.

Now that I have gotten the rights back to my book, I have improved my cover 100 fold. Now, with the new cover (which you can see by searching for my book on Amazon), it sells pretty well.

The point is, as I stated before, a bad cover will be the death of a book. So make sure you have a good one.

You'll notice I put this in the self-pub section and not the traditional publishing section. That's because with a publisher, you have next to no say what goes on the cover. The publishing companies have their "experts" who best know how to represent your book, down to the color (at least they think they do).

This is in self-publishing because getting the cover is completely up to you in this case.

If you are artistic, then you can create the cover all by yourself. That would be great, it can save you money, and you know you will be getting exactly what you want.

If, however, you are like most authors, you have been given the gift of the word and not the paintbrush. In this case, you will likely need to hire an artist.

Every front cover consists of three basic things: an image, a title, and the author's name. If you are creating only an ebook, a front cover is all you will need. However, if you are creating a book for print, you will also need a back cover and a spine designed. The spine will usually have the book title and the author's name on it. The back will have, at the very least, a description of the book and some image (even if it's only a couple of colors). It will also contain the UPC barcode and the ISBN number. So, you need to leave room for them in the bottom right corner of the back cover.

Overwhelmed yet? Don't be. Here's how we can make a cover nice and easy.

DO IT YOURSELF

I know I mentioned just a paragraph or two ago that you can't do it yourself without being an artist. That's not entirely true. Yes, unless you know something about creating art, you will not be able to finish this yourself, but we will start assuming you can.

"So, how can I make an eye-catching cover without knowing how to draw and paint?" you ask.

The answer is easy: Royalty Free Images.

There are several websites that have hundreds of thousands of images for you to download (for a price) that you can then use for whatever you wish.

So, why would you pay for images when there are millions of them for free just by doing a simple image search?

Again, an easy answer: Copyright.

By paying a few bucks for one of the images from one of the sites I listed below, you are getting a license to use that copyrighted image. Therefore, you cannot be sued. If you just use an image willy-nilly off a Google search, there is no guarantee the copyright owner of that image won't have their lawyers knocking on your door with cease and desist orders.

While there is nothing preventing you from using such images, you should play it safe. You have enough to worry about being an author than to have to worry about legal actions as well.

Anyway, here are a four sites I use to get my royalty-free images.

Big Stock Photo – https://www.bigstockphoto.com

Deposit Photos – https://www.depositphotos.com

Can Stock Photo – https://www.canstockphoto.com

123rf – https://www.123rf.com

There are other sites, but I have found that these ones have the greatest selection with the cheapest prices.

Just as long as you pay for the images, you can use it for your cover, and then if someone questions you about its use, all you have to do is show the receipt from the website saying that you have the legal use of the image. See? Protection is a good thing.

Just having the photo on your cover isn't enough. We also need the title and the author's name. If you're doing this through Createspace (for printing), there is a tool on the site that will allow you to add these. If not, then you are going to have to figure out a way to add them on your own. I suggest using a program like Adobe Photoshop, which will let you easily add text to your image. You need to choose a font that stands out, but doesn't overshadow the image. You also want the font to be large enough to be read in a thumbnail (small image), but not take over the whole cover. The same is true with the author name.

Your typical cover is going to be 6 inches x 9 inches (15.24cm x 22.86cm). You will also need a program like Photoshop in order to resize your image to around this size (or whatever size your final book is going to be).

If you can't get this done yourself, I suggest going on Fiverr (https://www.fiverr.com) and getting someone to do it for you for only $5. All you'd have to do is give them the image, the title, and author name, and they will create it for you. It is also possible to go to these people with no image at all and just describe what you're looking for. They will come up with something. And since it's only $5, you can actually hire a couple of the artists on this site and see who comes up with the best one. That will still be far cheaper than any other options I am going to present to you.

HIRING AN ARTIST
Sometimes the cover photo won't work. Or something the photo is a great starting point, but it needs more added to it.

PROMOTING YOUR BOOK

Whether you go the traditional route or decide to self-publish, you WILL have to promote your book. No one, not even your publisher, is going to promote it for you.

It sounds harsh, but it's true. Of course, a publisher is going to do *some* promotion of the book, but unless you're already an established best-seller, that is going to be very limited. Essentially, the only way to get it into the hands of your potential fans is to put the book into them yourself.

For many authors, they write their book easily, but this is the part that slips them up. This is where you need to switch over from your creative/artistic mindset, and adopt a business mindset. Think about what it takes to run a business (and keep it running). You need to worry about costs vs. profit. You need to have employees (maybe). You need to keep track of your profits for tax reasons. You must keep an inventory, and keep track of that inventory. And you need to advertise and promote your business.

Being an author and promoting your book works in much the same way as running a business. You have to account for a bunch of different things. The most important ones for an author are your costs, profits, and promotion. The reason why promotion is on this list is because if you don't get your book in front of people, no one is going to buy it. You can have the best book ever written in the history of the world, but if it sits on Amazon and no one sees it, no one will ever know.

So, once your book is written, edited, and published, your job is still not over. Now is the time to promote.

WHAT'S AN "AUTHOR PLATFORM"?

You will see the phrase "author platform" thrown around a lot online and in other books. The truth is, an author's platform is nothing more than your personal and professional connections, as well as all your media outlets (in other words, where you can sell your book), which would include your online presence—social media, website, etc.

Common platform building blocks include:

A website, or blog.

An e-newsletter.

Articles or columns you've written or currently write.

Guest contributions on websites.

Public speaking appearances.

Personal contacts (celebrities, publishers, radio/tv hosts).

A strong presence on Facebook, Twitter, Google+ and other social media outlets.

Memberships in professional organizations.

I wish I could tell you specifically how to build your own author platform. The fact is that this is not a "one size fits all" type of thing. Certainly .there are right and wrong things to do (see the next section). However, the platform depends on each individual person. What works for me is not necessarily going to work for you, too.

What I can tell you is that the most important thing for your platform is that you need to publish and distribute quality work and quality content to your target audience. This includes blog posts. This includes tweets on Twitter. If you aren't giving your audience quality material, you aren't going to get very far with your content. That's why the stuff mentioned in the previous sections and the stuff mentioned in the following sections are so important. Give the people good stuff and they are more likely to hang around.

THE RIGHT AND WRONG WAY TO PROMOTE YOUR BOOK ONLINE

In the old days, a person would write a book, they would go to a bookstore and have a book signing, they would talk about it on the radio, they would do readings at libraries, and that would be the extent of their promotions. Before anyone complains, I know that I am oversimplifying things. But these were the basics.

Now, if you have a book in print, you can still go and do some of these things, but because with the internet, you have a powerful weapon for promoting and selling your book. This can be more effective than going around and peddling the book from place to place. If you have published an ebook, online promotion may be your only choice.

I am not going to write about the same things that you can find everywhere else. Everyone will tell you, you need a Facebook page, you need a Twitter account, and you need a website. Yes, this stuff is true, however, if you don't already know this, and if you don't already have these things set up, you really aren't ready to promote your work.

Aside from those three things, you need to do more to get your work noticed. That's it. Because if you don't get up on your soapbox and tell people about your book, no one will ever know about it. Then, even though you have written the next *War and Peace* or *Catcher in the Rye*, even though your book could potentially be the next New York Times Bestseller, it will sit on the metaphorical Amazon shelf, collecting dust. But the question remains, how do I do it, and how to I do it the right way?

There are some things you can do. First thing: aside from your Twitter and Facebook (and actually using those accounts on a regular basis), you need to set up two other accounts. Amazon Author Central (https://authorcentral.amazon.com/) and Goodreads (http://www.goodreads.com/). Both of these sites will allow you to promote yourself as an author, as well as list your books where people can find them.

If you have an author page on Amazon, if someone searches your name (and in some cases something close to your name) your page will come up in the search. Also, if you have the Amazon page, people can click on your name when looking at any of your books and they will be able to see ALL of your books. Well worth the price—which is only about 15 minutes of your time to set up. You can also link your Facebook, Twitter, and website to this account, so that people can find you easily.

Goodreads works much the same way, allowing you to put all your books in one place. But Goodreads has some other features that will help you as well. You can have book giveaway on Goodreads. They suggest that you give away at least 10 books, but I have found it can be just as effective giving away two or three. What happens is people put your book on their virtual bookshelf in order to enter the contest. When I did my last one, I have almost 1,000 people enter the contest to win a copy of *The Leviathan Chronicles*. I gave away three books. So, for the cost of three of my own books, I was able to make 1,000 people aware that the book even existed. Will this translate into 1,000 sales—not a chance. But my book has now been placed on their shelves, and they might look at it one day and decide they are going to give it a shot. So, it is worth the small price.

Just don't set up these pages (Amazon and Goodreads), and forget about them. That is not going to do you any good. Be proactive, and keep them up to date. Otherwise, it's pointless even having them.

The other thing you want to do is get yourself some reviews. And though you're shooting for those 4 or 5 star reviews, you **NEVER** want to pay for a review. In case the uppercase, bold letters didn't get that point across the first time, I shall repeat it. You **NEVER** want to pay for a review.

So, why, you ask? Surely if you pay someone to give a review of your book, they are going to give you one of those much sought after 4 or 5 star reviews. The answer is, because it's dishonest. Would you want to purchase something if you found out that all the great things people said about it weren't true? No, probably not. Neither will your potential customers. So, yes, you want to solicit reviews. But the only cost to you should be a copy of your book.

The question remains, where do you go to get these reviews if you're not paying for them?

Goodreads is a great place to start. There are message boards on the website where you can post about your book and ask people for reviews in exchange for a free copy. You can also do a review exchange where you trade books with another author and write a review for them as they write a review for you. You can also get reviews by doing the giveaways mentioned earlier, but if you are doing that specifically for getting reviews, the number of books you giveaway should larger, because you will likely only see a 20 – 30% review rate on those giveaways (sometimes not even that much).

The other way is to email different book blogs and ask them for a review. Not only will they review your book on their blog, where all their fans will see it (and probably tweet about it), but they will usually post the review on Amazon and Goodreads where others will see it. Doing this can be quite time consuming. You will need to send out a personal email to each book blog you want to get a review from, which does take a bit of time.

Going back to Amazon, I cannot stress enough the power of the Amazon review. Amazon is probably the biggest bookseller in the world right now, and people are much more likely to buy a book that has been highly reviewed from an unknown author than if it has no reviews. So, make sure that gets done.

There are many more things you can do, but I would suggest starting here.

I will leave you with this one final thought. I follow others authors on Twitter, and what I notice many of them do is 20–30 times a day, they tweet about their book. This is annoying and it will lead to people unfollowing your account, which you don't want to happen. What it won't do is endear them to you enough to make them want to buy your book. Instead, on Twitter, only tweet about your book when you have something to tweet about (this goes for Facebook too). Tweet when you get your cover. Tweet when you begin a pre-order. Tweet when it's released. Tweet when you have a book giveaway. Tweet when you get a review. Don't just tweet over and over and over again how great your book is. It won't lead to anything.

BOOK BLOG TOURS

For most of us, gone are the days of doing an actual book tour, going from city to city across the country selling books in bookstores, doing book signings, and book talks. Even those of us published by a traditional publisher, unless you are Dan Brown, Stephen King or James Patterson, your publisher is not going to pay for you to go on tour. Even bestselling authors seem to be slowing down these sorts of tours, instead doing only a few spot tours in a section of the country near where they live.

So, if your publisher isn't going to pay for it, who do you think is going to foot the bill? If you guessed the author, you would be correct. Consider what a book tour would cost travelling across the country. You would need to pay for travel, hotel, and food. Even if you just stuck with those three things, a few city tours could end up costing you thousands of dollars. Think about how many books you would have to sell just to break even.

This is why largely book promotion, even for big name authors, has shifted away from these types of book tours to one a little closer to home and one that can be more far reaching: An Online Book Tour. Yes, you can still do that book tour, reach far and wide, and sell that book without ever leaving home. Now don't get me wrong, if you can set up book signings or speaking engagement at local stores, go for it. But forget about setting something up in a Barnes and Noble three states away unless you think that you'll be selling a few hundred or a thousand copies (which is hard to do in a couple of hours at a single book store).

So, what is a Book Blog Tour?

A Book Blog Tour, or Virtual Book Tour, is simply when an author is featured on a number of blogs in a set period of time.

Setting up a virtual book tour is easy, but it is time consuming. But it is no more time consuming (probably less so) than if you were to try setting up a book tour as described above.

STEP 1
First and foremost, consider your genre. Then try and find book blogs that fit your genre. I would start with these sites:

The Book Blogger List - https://bookbloggerlist.com/

The Book Blogger Directory - https://bookbloggerdirectory.wordpress.com/

Both of these websites have a pretty comprehensive list of blogs that are separated by genre. They aren't the only lists out there, but I have found both to be pretty good.

STEP 2

Look at the blogs and make a list of the ones you think will work well for your book. Include contact information for each blog.

STEP 3

What you want to do is then email each of those blogs telling them that you are preparing an online book tour and that you like their blog and you want your book to be on it. Describe the book for them and offer them a free copy (it can be an ebook), if they will allow you onto their blog.
Like with any other query of this type, some of the blogs will say yes, others will say no, and some won't respond at all. Don't get discouraged by the ones that don't respond or say they cannot put your book on. Instead, focus on the ones that said yes.

STEP 4

Set up dates for when you will be featured on their blog. It is best to keep these posts around the same time if possible. It has a greater impact and can generate more of a buzz if you can get three blogs (or more) to feature you in the same week.

There are a few different ways that you can be featured on a book blog:

A Review – This is by far the easiest to do, because there is no work involved. You send them your book, the blogger will read it, and then write an honest review of the book (if you ask them, they might even post the review on Amazon or Goodreads). The only thing is, that this doesn't necessarily mean they will give you a GOOD review. Keep that in mind. Most of these bloggers won't give you a BAD review (unless your book really is that horrible), but I have seen some of them give a 3-star review, which means that a book is only "OKAY."

If this happens, don't yell at the blogger, or try to defend your work. Simply thank them for the review and move on. Understand that no matter who you are, there are going to be people that don't like your book. Do you think that everyone who's read *Harry Potter* liked it? No, go on Amazon, there are a number of 1-star reviews for those books. Did that really affect the sales? No. So, as I said, thank them and move on. Remain professional.

An Interview – These can be fun. The blogger will give you a list of questions to answer, and you answer them. Yup, it's that simple.

Or is it?

Yes, all an interview consists of is a list of questions for you to answer. But you can't give simplistic answers. Think about what the purpose of a book blog is: to inform readers about books and to entertain them. If your interviewer asks, "What inspired you to write this book?" your answer needs to be more than, "My wife and daughter." Yes, it's fine to say that your wife and daughter inspired your book, however, you need to elaborate. How did they inspire you? What occurred? What are their thoughts on your book now that it's done? You need to give in depth answers to these questions.

But, don't go overboard. Don't write a three page response that is going to make the blogger's reader's minds explode. They are simply not going to read the interview. Look at an interview in a magazine with a celebrity. Look at the length of their answers. They vary from a couple of sentences to a couple paragraphs. Your responses should be the same.

In an interview, always remember to have the blogger plug the book you are promoting, as well as your website, Twitter, Facebook, etc.

A Guest Post – A guest post can be fun. Essentially, when you write a guest post, you are taking over the blog for a day and writing a post.

Generally, the blogger will give you a topic, or a list of topics to write about. Then, you take their idea and you do a blog post about it. Sometimes, they will just tell you to write about anything, or give you a genre (like if you're on a horror blog, it might be something to do with horror, or for a romance blog, the same thing). Generally they are looking for a post of about 400–500 words, but this will depend on the blogger. You write the post, they will post it on the blog, and link you in the post.

Your post, no matter what the topic, should be engaging. If it isn't engaging, if it is boring to read, then no one is going to read it. Think about the audience you are trying to reach with your book. Hopefully, those same people are going to be reading the blog, so you want to write for that audience. Engage that audience. If you can do that, you'll have a good blog post.

If you can put a little plug in there for the book you are promoting, all the better. But if you do nothing but promote your book, then that is not only going to be boring, but will annoy your potential audience and make them click off the post before they read it all—not what we want.

Look back through this book. Some of these sections actually started out as guest blog posts. I do mention my books, but I do so in the context of what I'm writing. I also don't beat you over the head with it. Because doing that is like me jumping up on a tree stump and shouting, "BUY MY BOOK! BUY MY BOOK!" It is also a bad way to try and promote yourself.

STEP 5

Once your post is live your job isn't done. Now you want to promote the post itself. Post the link to the blog on your Twitter, Facebook, Google+, etc. Get people to go to the blog and check it out. If you have an email list, send it out on there as well (though if you are getting a few posts over a week, consider emailing all the links at once instead of each individually. Sending out too many emails is a good way to lose potential customers).
Remember the more people that see the blog post are more potential fans of your work.

STEP 6

The last step is to check back on the blogs for comments or questions about your review, or interview, or guest post, and respond to them. Like on Facebook or Twitter, it's not enough to just post something and forget it. You need to engage with your audience. This is the way you are going to sell books.

HIRE SOMEONE

If you don't feel comfortable, or confident enough to go it alone, you can hire someone to set it all up for you.

While they won't write the blog post, or conduct the interview for you, they will pretty much handle everything else. They will get a list of bloggers, they will send out the copies of your book, they will schedule everything to happen over a week or two. They will remind you when things are coming up so you don't miss a deadline.

Of course, with the convenience of having these things done for you, you will be sacrificing time for money. Yes, it will cost you some money for this, but if you don't feel like you can do it alone, then this could be money well spent.

Here is a list of a couple of these Virtual Book Tour sites that will help get you on blogs. I have used the first two myself and had decent results with them (the others have good reviews). Prices can range from $25 for some of the cheapest tours, to $400 for some of the most expensive. I have never done any of the really expensive ones and usually stick to the ones that cost between $100-200, and have had good results with them. Some of these will also offer other services, such as getting reviews on Amazon. I have never used these services, but that will be up to you to try if you so desire.

Here is the list:

Goddess Fish Promotions - https://www.goddessfish.com/

Sage Blog Tours - https://www.sagesblogtours.com/

Enchanted Book Promotions - https://www.enchantedbookpromotions.com/

Tasty Book Tours - https://www.tastybooktours.com/

There are others. No matter what, do your homework before you commit to anything. Look at the blogs these promoters typically get their books on. You don't want to submit your sci-fi book if mostly where they put books are romance blogs. It would be like trying to sell sand in the desert. In other words, it isn't going to do anybody any good.

Whether you go it alone, or you pay someone to do it for you, I do suggest these virtual book tours.

They are a good tool to get your book in front of an audience. The more places your book is featured, the more likely something is going to come up if someone happens to Google your name. And it lends a bit of credibility to you and your project.

THE "REAL-LIFE" BOOK TOUR

BOOK FAIRS & FESTIVALS

I know I just went out there and told you that going out and doing live book signings was a waste of time. Book fairs and festivals are the exception to this rule.

If you are going to travel to promote your book, you have to weigh your expense vs. your profit. Think about your typical bookstore, even a big one like Barnes and Noble in a big city. A Barnes and Noble might see a couple thousand people come through the doors on a busy weekend, many of those people (let's estimate that it's close to 60%) already have the book they want to purchase in mind (if they are even there to purchase a book). The remaining people are just browsing the shelves for something new to read. Of those remaining 40%, you might sell your book to about 5% if you are on your feet and actively putting your book into their hands. Now if you figure you're there for the entire day (which usually you're only scheduled at a bookstore for a few hours) you might see 2,000 people pass through the doors. The 40% that don't know what they're looking for would mean 800 potential customers and 5% of that would mean you've sold 40 books. And that's being generous.

Now consider a Book Festival. These are usually open to the public for free. Some of these festivals can see thousands of people. And a much higher percentage of these people are looking for something new to read. Assuming you can sell to the same 5% of people that come up to you, you are looking at a much higher sales margin (plus, the bookstore isn't taking a cut of your profit).

The tables at these book festivals usually aren't free (unless you are a big name author who is guaranteed to draw a crowd). They can range in price from anywhere from $25 (that's the cheapest I've ever paid for a table) to $400 (most expensive table I've ever seen).

Now, even for these, I don't generally travel too far, and if you do plan on travelling for one of these events, you need to consider the cost of the table and the travel costs. Yes, it might only cost $25 for a table at one of these events, but if it's going to cost you another $100 in gas to drive there, and you need to get a hotel for the night. That's another $100, then you are looking at a total cost of $225. Think about that before you decide on anything.

As I said, I generally don't travel too far. Essentially, if the event is within driving distance of my house, I will consider it. Driving distance for you depends wholly on your own preferences. For me, the limit is generally six hours away by car. If it's further than that, I generally won't do it.

That being said, I have done events far from home. Now, the reason I have participated in them is because they happened while we were on family vacations. If I have to sacrifice one of my vacation days with my family to sell some books, then I'm fine with that. If I'm in the area already while the event is happening, I'm all for it. Then, the expense of travel is negated mainly because you are travelling for leisure (which you would have done anyway). An added bonus is that because you are also travelling for business, you can write off (some of) the travel expenses on your taxes.

Here are some of the more popular Book Fairs and Festivals. There is at least one in every state. So if you can find on near you, try attending it with your book. See how you do. If it works, then go again, if not, look for other festivals nearby.

For lists of Book Festivals –

Book Reporter – https://www.bookreporter.com/book-festivals

Library of Congress – https://www.read.gov/resources/statefairs.php

Some of the Better Book Festivals –

Gaithersburg Book Festival – https://www.gaithersburgbookfestival.org

Baltimore Book Festival – https://www.baltimorebookfestival.com

New York Book Festival – https://www.newyorkbookfesitval.com

Hudson Children's Book Festival – https://www.hudsonchildrensbookfestival.com

Northwest Book Festival – https://www.nwbookfestival.com

Collingswood Book Festival – https://www.collingswoodbookfestival.com

Mississippi Book Festival – https://www.msbookfestival.com

Miami Book Fair – https://www.miamibookfair.com

Bay Area Book Festival – https://www.baybookfest.org

OTHER VENUES

Book fairs and festivals aren't the only venues that you can try.

Craft Fairs

Personally, and it might sound strange, I have had some success doing local craft fairs. It works because you have a product that you created, plus there are few, if any, other people at these types of shows also selling books. Most local shows cost less than $50 for a table. You would only need to sell a few books to make the cost back, and because it's local, travel expenses are minimal.

To find local book fairs look at your local town, city, county or state websites for a calendar of events. They usually list fairs like these on these calendars and will give you the contact info of the people running it. Many of these local events are run by clubs and organizations and generally don't have websites dedicated specifically for the event. Some of them are listed on the websites below.

There are some larger craft fairs out there, these generally are a little more expensive. I have only ever attended one of these larger craft fairs, but I was still pleasantly surprised at the turnout.

Here are two sites that list a good deal of these craft fairs. They both have search engines on their site to find festivals, but they also have the ability to look at a particular state.

Festival Net – https://www.festivalnet.com

Fairs and Festivals – https://www.fairsandfestivals.net

Conventions

The genre of your book can also open doors to other venues. Just about every genre has a convention. These are good to go to as an author, because there are people there who love and are looking to get your specific kind of book. The most popular ones are sci-fi and comic conventions. Some of the larger ones see over 100,000 people attending each year.

Here are just a few of the conventions across the country for each genre. To find others, just do a simple Google search for them.

Romance –
Romance Novel Convention – https://www.romancenovelconvention.com

Authors After Dark – https://www.authorsafterdark.org

RWA Annual Conference – https://www.rwa.org/conference

Horror –
Monster-Mania Con – https://www.monstermania.net

Horror Realm – https://www.horrorrealmcon.com

World Horror Convention – https://www.worldhorrorconvention.com

Crypticon – https://www.crypticonseattle.com

Mystery –
Bouchercon – https://www.bouchercon.info

Sleuthfest – https://www.sleuthfest.com

Nancy Drew Conference – https://www.ndsleuths.com/ndsconventions.html

Thrillerfest – https://www.thrillerfest.com

Fantasy –
World Fantasy Convention – https://www.worldfantasy.org

Dragon Con – https://www.dragoncon.org

Science Fiction –

Balticon – https://www.balticon.org

TusCon – https://www.tusconscificon.com

Intergalactic Expo – https://www.intergalacticexpo.com

ConCarolinas – https://www.concarolinas.org

Young Adult –
YallFest – https://www.yallfest.org

Literary –
ReaderCon – https://www.readercon.org

Libertycon – https://www.libertycon.org

Believe me, this is just the tip of the iceberg. I wish I could go into this and give you the hundreds that I know about. For more, just do some Google searches and you'll get an extensive list.

WHAT TO DO

Whether it is a book festival, a craft fair, or a convention, you can't just set your books out and sit there like a lump all day waiting for people to come to you and give you money. It doesn't work like that. Keep in mind that at any of these places, there are hundreds of other vendors competing for people's time and money, and these people are walking around from table to table looking at hundreds of different things.

To be sure, you can get some sales sitting passively at your table. But you will get even more sales by actively engaging people as they walk by. Call out to them, say hello, compliment their dress or shirt, anything that will get them to come over to you. I've even seen people shout out, "Let me tell you about my book!" Yes, for those of us who are introverted, this is not going to be an easy task, but it is something you need to do if you want to be successful at this. You can easily double your sales just by engaging people as they pass your booth.

That logline we spoke about earlier? Memorize it. This is going to be the selling point for your book. Once you have their attention, you have only a short amount of time to really grab them. Tell the person your logline. A good deal of people will comment on it. That's when you swoop in and tell them more about the book. Now you have them engaged, and now you can potentially make a sale.

While you are talking to them, it is always good to hand them a copy. If they have something physical in their hands, it gives them something to connect to. They will flip through it, read the back, and decide if they want it or not. Remember, the worst that can happen is they give it back to you. Yes, I know what you're thinking. You think the real worst thing is they could run off with your book. I'd agree with you, but after doing this for seven years I can attest that this has never happened to me, and I hand people my books a lot.

Another thing that people overlook: A tablecloth. Think about this, what is more attractive to the eye, a gray folding table or a table covered by a nice, clean tablecloth? If you said the gray folding table, then you really need to have your head examined. Of course it's the tablecloth. Most of these places will give you a very plain table that is not at all attractive. If it doesn't look attractive, we are going to pass it by. So, do yourself a favor, invest in a $10 tablecloth to cover your table. Most tables are 6 feet long at fairs and festivals, so get one that would cover that length.

Another eye catcher is a sign or banner. These are great to bring people over. Put your book cover (or covers) on the sign. People will see your book cover even if they aren't near your table. It is a way to engage someone before you even have to say a word. Banners can be pricy, I have found that the best place to get a banner (and the quality is pretty good too) is VistaPrint (https://www.vistaprint.com). They usually run sales where you can get a six foot banner for around $40. Not a bad deal.

Speaking of VistaPrint, I also go to them to get business cards. This is something you should have anyway, but they are a necessity at festivals and conventions. Make sure your name and contact information are on them, as well as a website where they can find out other information about your book.

GET CREATIVE

Seriously, if you're a writer, this should be the part you're good at.

The point is, I could give you a thousand different ways to promote yourself and your book. There will always be ways I don't think of. If you think of other ways, try them—especially if they're free. If it works, great! Keep doing it. If it doesn't work, try something else. The only limit on promoting yourself is your own imagination.

DON'T FALL FOR IT

Lastly, there are many companies out there that will "guarantee" exposure for your book. They will promise you a thousand different things and tell you that they will get you on the *New York Times Bestseller List*. Be wary of these places.

Remember, there are no guarantees. What works for one author is not going to work for another. There is no formula that will work every time. If someone is guaranteeing you something for your money, you better get it in writing, because if they don't follow through, you might have some trouble getting your money back.

That's all I have for you. Now get out there and write... and of course, promote your books!

WEBSITES & RESOURCES

All of the websites listed here are listed somewhere in this book. They are in no particular order, I just thought having them all in one place would be best. I've included a couple of extra ones on here not mentioned above, just because I think they might be pertinent and helpful.

Preditors & Editors – https://www.pred-ed.com

Fiverr – https://www.fiverr.com

Upwork – https://www.upwork.com

Everyone Who's Anyone – https://www.everyonewhosanyone.com

Createspace – https://www.createspace.com

Smashwords – https://www.smashwords.com

Goodreads – https://www.goodreads.com

Kindle Direct Publishing - https://kdp.amazon.com/

Smashwords – https://www.smashwords.com

Amazon Author Central - https://authorcentral.amazon.com/

The Book Blogger List - https://bookbloggerlist.com/

The Book Blogger Directory - https://bookbloggerdirectory.wordpress.com/

Goddess Fish Promotions - https://www.goddessfish.com/

Sage Blog Tours - https://www.sagesblogtours.com/

Enchanted Book Promotions - https://www.enchantedbookpromotions.com/

Tasty Book Tours - https://www.tastybooktours.com/

Romance Novel Convention – https://www.romancenovelconvention.com

Authors After Dark – https://www.authorsafterdark.org

RWA Annual Conference – https://www.rwa.org/conference

Monster-Mania Con – https://www.monstermania.net

Horror Realm – https://www.horrorrealmcon.com

World Horror Convention – https://www.worldhorrorconvention.com

Crypticon – https://www.crypticonseattle.com

Bouchercon – https://www.bouchercon.info

Sleuthfest – https://www.sleuthfest.com

Nancy Drew Conference – https://www.ndsleuths.com/ndsconventions.html

Thrillerfest – https://www.thrillerfest.com

World Fantasy Convention – https://www.worldfantasy.org

Dragon Con – https://www.dragoncon.org

Balticon – https://www.balticon.org

TusCon – https://www.tusconscificon.com

Intergalactic Expo – https://www.intergalacticexpo.com

ConCarolinas – https://www.concarolinas.org

YallFest – https://www.yallfest.org

ReaderCon – https://www.readercon.org

Libertycon – https://www.libertycon.org

Google Maps – https://maps.google.com

Other Books by James Mascia

All Available on Kindle, Nook, iPad or any e-reading Device

Short Stories –
The Collector
City of Darkness
High School Heroes: Cold Lies
High School Heroes: Rescue Mission
High School Heroes: The Guardian
High School Heroes: Imagination
High School Heroes: Secrets of the Past
Even Heroes Have the Right to Bleed
The Leviathan Chronicles: The Last Stand at Aeprion

Novels –
High School Heroes
High School Heroes II: Camp Hero
High School Heroes III: Hero Heist
High School Heroes IV: Hero's Burden
High School Heroes V: Heroic Acts
The Island of Dren
Urban Jungle

Graphic Novels –
High School Heroes: Volume 1
The Poe Murders
Plan 10 From Outer Space (Coming Soon)

Non-Fiction -
1,100 Ways to Write Your Story

About the Author

James Mascia is the author of many great young adult books, including his wonderfully reviewed series, *High School Heroes*. When James isn't writing, he is teaching English and Literature in a high school in Maryland. When he isn't writing or teaching, he usually dons a black mask and hops around from rooftop to rooftop, making the world a better place for all.

His wife and son are very tolerant of him, especially when he drags them around to many sci-fi and comic conventions.

www.ingramcontent.com/pod-product-compliance
Lightning Source LLC
Chambersburg PA
CBHW081658270326
41933CB00017B/3211